THE FALL
OF
BRITISH TYRANNY
By JOHN LEACOCK

JOHN LEACOCK

Among the elusive figures of early American Drama stands John Leacock, author of "The Fall of British Tyranny,"[1] published in 1776, in Philadelphia. Even more elusive is the identification, inasmuch as his name has been spelled variously Leacock, Lacock, and Laycock. To add to the confusion, Watson's "Annals of Philadelphia," on the reminiscent word of an old resident of that town, declares that Joseph Leacock penned "The Medley."[2] "He wrote also a play, with good humour," says this authority, "called 'British Tyranny.'" On careful search of the files, no definite information in regard to Leacock has been forthcoming. The dedication to "The Fall of British Tyranny" was signed "Dick Rifle," but there is no information to be traced from this pseudonym.

Searching the Colonial Records of Pennsylvania, I discovered no less than three John Leacocks mentioned, all of whom were Coroners, as well as a Joseph Leacock, who occupied the same position. Examining the Records of the Pennsylvania Soldiers of the Revolution, I found several John Leacocks in the ranks as privates, and also one John Laycock.

Professor Moses Coit Tyler, in his "Literary History of the American Revolution" (ii, 198), giving a list of the characters in the play and the names of those supposed to be lampooned, analyzes the piece thoroughly, and says, "From internal evidence, it must be inferred that the writing of the play was finished after the publication of 'Common Sense' in January, 1776, and before the news had reached Philadelphia of the evacuation of Boston, March 17, 1776." Though Sabin takes for granted that Leacock wrote "The Fall of British Tyranny," Hildeburn, [Pg 280]in the "Issues of the Press" (ii, 249), states that it is "said to have been written by Mr. Laycock of Philadelphia." If the John Leacock, whose name appears in the Philadelphia Directory of 1802, is the one who wrote "The Fall of British Tyranny," following that clue we find his name disappearing from the Directory in 1804. Hence, he must either have died, or have moved away from Philadelphia.

The elusive name of Leacock is to be considered also in connection with an opera entitled, "The Disappointment; or, The Force of Credulity," signed by Andrew Barton,[3] supposed to be a pseudonym, and attributed variously to "Colonel" Thomas Forrest and to John Leacock. I already have had occasion to mention "The Disappointment" in connection with Godfrey's "The Prince of Parthia." The reader will remember that in 1767 "The Disappointment" was put into rehearsal, but was suddenly withdrawn in preference to Godfrey's piece. This play has been fully and interestingly analyzed by O. G. Sonneck, who gives the reasons for the withdrawal of the play from rehearsal by the American Company of Philadelphia, 1767. These reasons are definitely stated in the *Pennsylvania Gazette* for April 16, 1767, which contains this warning in the American Company's advertisement of "The Mourning Bride": "N.B. 'The Disappointment' (that was advertised for Monday), as it contains personal Reflections, is unfit for the Stage."

The reason why this piece is attributed to "Colonel" Thomas Forrest is that there is a memorandum in substantiation on the title-page of a copy owned by the Library Company of Philadelphia.

Mr. Sonneck gives further and more extensive treatment of the subject in his excellent book on "Early Opera in America," (Schirmer, 1915) as well as in "Sammelbände der Internationale Musik Gesellschaft," for 1914-1915.

We mention the matter here, because, although Sonneck enters into a long discussion of the life of Forrest, he fails to give any satisfactory account of John Leacock. In fact, he says in closing, "If Andrew Barton, Esq., is to be a pseudonym, it seems [Pg 281]to me that John Leacock, claimed (by Mr. Hildeburn) to have written the tragi-comedy of 'The Fall of British Tyranny,' should not be cast aside so cheerfully in favour of Thomas Forrest."

Seilhamer and Durang, referring to the matter, mention Joseph Leacock as a claimant for the authorship of "The Disappointment," and say that he was a jeweler and a silversmith in Philadelphia; they also mention John Leacock, the Coroner. Durang, in the "History of the Philadelphia Stage," throws all weight in favour of Thomas Forrest. Sonneck says further, regarding the matter,—"We may dispose of Joseph by saying that he seems to have been among the dead when, in 1796, the second edition of 'The Disappointment,' revised and corrected by the author, was issued. On the other hand, Coroner John Leacock figures in the Philadelphia Directories even later."

So the matter stands. The play, however, is a very definite contribution, illustrating how quickly the American spirit changed in the days preceding the Revolution. Imagine, in 1762, the students of the College of New Jersey giving a piece entitled "The Military Glory of Great Britain;"[4] and so short a time afterwards, only fourteen years, in fact, a piece with the title, "The Fall of British Tyranny," being greeted by the theatre-going public! Leacock's attempt may be taken as the first example that we have of an American chronicle play. And it is likewise significant as being the first literary piece in which George Washington appears as a character. In the advertisement, the play is thus described (see Ford):

"A pleasing scene between Roger and Dick, two shepherds near Lexington.

"Clarissa, etc. A very moving scene on the death of Dr. Warren, etc., in a chamber near Boston, the morning after the battle of Bunker's Hill.

"A humorous scene between the Boatswain and a Sailor on board a man-of-war, near Norfolk in Virginia.

"Two very laughable scenes between the Boatswain, two Sailors and the Cook, exhibiting specimens of seafaring oratory, and peculiar eloquence of those sons of Neptune, touching Tories, Convicts, and Black Regulars: and between Lord Kidnapper and the Boatswain.

[Pg 282]

"A very black scene between Lord Kidnapper and Major Cudjo.

"A religious scene between Lord Kidnapper, Chaplain, and the Captain.

"A scene, the Lord Mayor, etc., going to St. James's with the address.

"A droll scene, a council of war in Boston, Admiral Tombstone, Elbow Room, Mr. Caper, General Clinton and Earl Piercy.

"A diverting scene between a Whig and a Tory.

"A spirited scene between General Prescott and Colonel Allen.

"A shocking scene, a dungeon, between Colonel Allen and an officer of the guard.

"Two affecting scenes in Boston after the flight of the regulars from Lexington, between Lord Boston, messenger and officers of the guard.

"A patriotic scene in the camp at Cambridge, between the Generals Washington, Lee, and Putnam, etc., etc."

It is interesting to note that in the Abbé Robin's discerning remarks, concerning the effect of drama on the pupils of Harvard in 1781, and on the general appeal of drama among the American Patriots, he mentions "The Fall of British Tyranny" without giving the author's name.

FOOTNOTES:

[1]The Fall/of/British Tyranny;/or,/American Liberty/Triumphant./The First Campaign./A Tragi-Comedy of Five Acts,/as Lately Planned/at the Royal Theatrum Pandemonium,/at St. James's./The Principal Place of Action in America./Publish'd According to Act of Parliament./Quis furor ô cives! quæ tanta licentia ferri?/Lucan. lib. I. ver. 8./What blind, detested madness could afford/Such horrid licence to the murd'ring sword?/Rowe./Philadelphia:/Printed by Styner and Cist, in Second-street,/near Arch-street. M DCC LXXVI.

[2]"The Medley; or, Harlequin Have At Ye All." A pantomime produced at Covent Garden, and published in 1778.

[3]From Sabin, I take the following:

BARTON (A.) "The Disappointment; or, The Force of Credulity." A new American Comic Opera, of two Acts. By Andrew Barton, Esq. [Motto.] *New York, Printed in the year* M, DCC, LXVIII. 8vo. pp. v., 58. P. t. Second edition, revised and corrected, with large additions, by the

Author. *Philadelphia*, Francis Shallus, 1796. 12 mo. pp. iv., 94, p. 3801. |Sabin also notes that the Philadelphia Library copy is very rare, with MS Key to the characters, who were Philadelphians. Air No. iv is Yankee Doodle (1767).|

[4] The Title-page runs as follows:

The/Military Glory/of/Great-Britain,/an/Entertainment,/given by the late Candidates for/Bachelor's Degree,/At the close of the/Anniversary Commencement, held/in/Nassau-Hall/New-Jersey/September 29th, 1762./Philadelphia:/Printed by William Bradford, M, DCC, LXII.

[Pg 283]

FAC-SIMILE TITLE-PAGE OF THE FIRST EDITION

[Pg 285]

THE DEDICATION

To Lord Boston, Lord Kidnapper, and the innumerable and never-ending Clan of Macs and Donalds upon Donalds, and the Remnant of the Gentlemen Officers, Actors, Merry Andrews, strolling Players, Pirates, and Buccaneers in America.

My Lords and Gentlemen:

Understanding you are vastly fond of plays and farces, and frequently exhibit them for your own amusement, and the laudable purpose of ridiculing your masters (the YANKEES, as you call 'em), it was expected you would have been polite enough to have favoured the world, or America at least (at whose expense you act them), with some of your play-bills, or with a sample of your composition.

I shall, however, not copy your churlishness, but dedicate the following Tragi-Comedy to your patronage, and for your future entertainment; and as the most of you have already acted your particular parts of it, both comic and tragic, in reality at Lexington, Bunker's-Hill, the Great-Bridge, &c., &c., &c., to the very great applause of yourselves, tho' not of the whole house, no doubt you will preserve the marks, or memory of it, as long as you live, as it is wrote in capital American characters and letters of blood on your posteriors: And however some Whigs may censure you for your affected mirth (as they term it, in the deplorable situation you are now in, like hogs in a pen, and in want of elbow room), yet I can by no means agree with them, but think it a proof of true heroism and philosophy, to endeavour to make the best of a bad bargain, and laugh at yourselves, to prevent others from laughing at you; and tho' you are deprived of the use of your teeth, it is no reason you should be bereaved of the use of your tongues, your eyes, your ears, and your risible faculties and powers. That would be cruel indeed! after the glorious and fatiguing campaign you have made, and the many signal victories obtained over whole herds of cattle and swine, routing flocks of sheep, lambs and geese, storming hen-roosts, and taking them prisoners, and thereby raising the glory of Old England[Pg 286] *to a pitch she never knew before. And ye Macs, and ye Donalds upon Donalds, go on, and may our gallows-hills and liberty poles be honour'd and adorn'd with some of your heads: Why should Tyburn and Temple-bar make a monopoly of so valuable a commodity?*

Wishing you abundance of entertainment in the re-acting this Tragi-Comedy, and of which I should be proud to take a part with you, tho' I have reason to think you would not of choice let me come within three hundred yards of your stage, lest I should rob you of your laurels, receive the clap of the whole house, and pass for a second Garrick among you, as you know I always act with applause, speak bold—point blank—off hand—and without prompter.

I am, My Lords and Gentlemen Buffoons,
Your always ready humble servant,
DICK RIFLE.

[Pg 287]

THE PREFACE

Solomon said, "Oppression makes a wise man mad:" but what would he have said, had he lived in these days, and seen the oppression of the people of Boston, and the distressed situation of the inhabitants of Charlestown, Falmouth, Stonnington, Bristol, Norfolk, &c.? Would he not have said, "The tongue of the sucking child cleaveth to the roof in his mouth for thirst; the young children ask for bread, but no man breaketh it unto them?" "They that did feed delicately, perish in the streets; they that were brought up in scarlet, embrace the dung." What would he have said of rejected petitions, disregarded supplications, and contemned remonstrances? Would he not have said, "From hardness of heart, good Lord, deliver us?" What would he have said of a freeborn people butchered—their towns desolated, and become an heap of ashes—their inhabitants become beggars, wanderers and vagabonds—by the cruel orders of an unrelenting tyrant, wallowing in luxury, and wantonly wasting the people's wealth, to oppress them the more? Would he not have said, it was oppression and ingratitude in the highest degree, exceeding the oppression of the children of Israel? and, like Moses, have cried out, let the people go? Would he not have wondered at our patience and long-suffering, and have said, "'Tis time to change our master!—'Tis time to part!"—And had he been an American born, would he not have shewed his wisdom by adopting the language of independency? Happy then for America in these fluctuating times, she is not without her Solomons, who see the necessity of heark'ning to reason, and listening to the voice of COMMON SENSE.[Pg 288]

THE GODDESS OF LIBERTY

Hail! Patriots,[5] hail! by me inspired be!Speak boldly, think and act for Liberty,United sons, America's choice band,Ye Patriots firm, ye sav'ours of the land.Hail! Patriots, hail! rise with the rising sun,Nor quit your labour, till the work is done.Ye early risers in your country's cause,Shine forth at noon, for Liberty and Laws.Build a strong tow'r, whose fabric may endureFirm as a rock, from tyranny secure.Yet would you build my fabric to endure,Be your hearts warm—but let your hands be pure.Never to shine, yourselves, your country sell;But think you nobly, while in place act well.Let no self-server general trust betray,No picque, no party, bar the public way.Front an arm'd world, with union on your side:No foe shall shake you—if no friends divide.At night repose, and sweetly take your rest;None sleeps so sound as those by conscience blest;May martyr'd patriots whisper in your ear,To tread the paths of virtue without fear;May pleasing visions charm your patriot eyes;While Freedom's sons shall hail you blest and wise,Hail! my last hope, she cries, inspired by me,Wish, talk, write, fight, and die—for LIBERTY.

FOOTNOTES:

[5] The Congress

[Pg 289]

THE PROLOGUE

Spoken by Mr. Peter Buckstail.

Since 'tis the fashion, preface, prologue next,Else what's a play?—like sermon without text!Since 'tis the fashion then, I'll not oppose;For what's a man if he's without a nose?The curtain's up—the music's now begun,What is 't—Why murder, fire, and sword, and gun.What scene?—Why blood!—What act?—Fight and be free!Or be ye slaves—and give up liberty!Blest Continent, while groaning nations roundBend to the servile yoke, ignobly bound,May ye be free—nor ever be opprest By murd'ring tyrants, but a land of rest!What say ye to 't? what says the audience?Methinks I hear some whisper COMMON SENSE.Hark! what say them Tories?—Silence—let 'em speak,Poor fools! dumb—they hav'n't spoke a word this week,Dumb let 'em be, at full end of their tethers,'Twill save the expense of tar and of feathers:Since old Pluto's lurch'd 'em, and swears he does not knowIf more these Tory puppy curs will bark or no.Now ring the bell—Come forth, ye actors, come,The Tragedy's begun, beat, beat the drum,Let's all advance, equipt like volunteers,Oppose the foe, and banish all our fears.

We will be free—or bravely

we will die,

>And leave to Tories tyrants'

legacy,

>And all our share of its

dependency.

[Pg 290]

DRAMATIS PERSONÆ

LORD PARAMOUNT,	Mr. Bute.
LORD MOCKLAW,	Mr. Mansfield.
LORD HYPOCRITE,	Mr. Dartmouth.
LORD POLTRON,	Mr. Sandwich.
LORD CATSPAW,	Mr. North.
LORD WISDOM,	Mr. Chatham.
LORD RELIGION,	Bishop of St. Asaph.
LORD JUSTICE,	Mr. Camden.
LORD PATRIOT,	Mr. Wilkes.
BOLD IRISHMAN,	Mr. Burke.
JUDAS,	Mr. Hutchinson.
CHARLEY,	Mr. Jenkinson.
BRAZEN,	Mr. Wedderburne.
COLONEL,	Mr. Barre.
LORD BOSTON,	Mr. Gage.
ADMIRAL TOMBSTONE,	Mr. Graves.
ELBOW ROOM,[6]	Mr. Howe.
MR. CAPER,	Mr. Burgoyne.
LORD KIDNAPPER,	Mr. Dunmore.
GENERAL WASHINGTON.	
GENERAL LEE.	
GENERAL PUTNAM.	

Officers, Soldiers, Sailors, Citizens, Negroes, &c., &c., &c.

FOOTNOTES:

[6]It seems to be generally thought that the expression of "Elbow Room" is to be attributed to General Howe, and not to General Burgoyne.

[Pg 291]

THE FALL
OF
BRITISH TYRANNY, &c.
ACT I.

LORD PARAMOUNT [*solus, strutting about*].

Many long years have rolled delightfully on, whilst I have been basking in the sunshine of grandeur and power, whilst I have imperceptibly (tho' not unsuspected) guided the chariot of state, and greased with the nation's gold the imperial wheels.

'Tis I that move the mighty engine of royalty, and with the tincture of my somniferous opiate or (in the language of a courtier) by the virtue of my secret influence, I have lulled the axletree to sleep, and brought on a pleasing insensibility.

Let their champion, Lord Wisdom, groan, he is now become feeble and impotent, a mere cripple in politics; their Lord Patriot's squint has lost its basilisk effect: and the bold Irishman may bellow the *Keenew* till he's hoarse, he's no more when compar'd to me than an Irish salmon to a Scotch herring: I care not a bawbee for them all. I'll reign in Britain, I'll be king of their counsels, and chief among the princes.

Oh! ambition, thou darling of my soul! stop not till I rise superior to all superlative, till I mount triumphantly the pinnacle of glory, or at least open the way for one of my own family and name to enter without opposition.

The work is now cut out, and must be finish'd, I have ventur'd too far to recede, my honour's at stake, my importance, nay my life, depends upon it!

Last night's three hours' closeting has effectually done the business; then I spoke my mind in such terms as to make a lasting impression, never to be eradicated—all—all was given up[Pg 292] to me, and now since I hold the reins of government, since I am possessed of supreme power, every thing shall be subservient to my royal will and pleasure.

SCENE II.
Enter MOCKLAW.

MOCKLAW. I am your Lordship's most obedient humble servant.

PARAMOUNT. Be seated,—I sent for you to have a small conference with you—and to let you know, your advice respecting certain points of law, I have found succeeded to admiration; even beyond my most sanguine expectations.

MOCKLAW. I am heartily glad of it, altho' the advice I gave your Lordship, I cannot say, was law; yet, your Lordship can easily pass it as such by a royal proclamation: and should it ever be disputed, I have quirks and quibbles enough at your service, with Mr. Brazen and Mr. Attorney-General's assistance, to render it so doubtful, obscure and ambiguous, as to puzzle Lord Justice, perplex Dunning, and confound Glynn.

PARAMOUNT. Can you show me an instance of a royal proclamation passing for a law? or advise me how to make it such, if you can, I shall make it well worth your study.

MOCKLAW. My Lord, as you have now got a parliament exactly to your mind, ev'ry thing you propose will be granted; but in order that you may see precedents are not wanting—there is a statute in the reign of Henry the 8th that expressly shews the then parliament passed a law that the king's proclamation should be the law of the land—

PARAMOUNT. Are you sure of that?

MOCKLAW. My Lord, here it is—this is real law: *Luce meridiana clariora.* When we find any thing of this kind, ready made to our hands, it's a treasure we should never part with.

[PARAMOUNT *reads.*

PARAMOUNT. I see it plain! this, this alone is worth a ton of gold.—Now, by St. Andrew! I'll strike a stroke that shall surprise all Europe, and make the boldest of the adverse party turn pale and tremble—Scotch politics, Scotch intrigues, Scotch influence, and Scotch impudence (as they have termed it), they shall see ere long shine with unheard of splendour, and the name of Lord Paramount the mighty, shall blaze in the annals of[Pg 293] the world with far greater lustre (as a consummate politician) than the name of Alexander the Great, as an hero!

MOCKLAW. That day I much wish for,—but, with your Lordship's permission, I would just mention, that secrecy and dissimulation are the soul of enterprise; your Lordship hath many enemies, who watch ev'ry movement of state with a jealous and wary eye.

PARAMOUNT. I know it, but the futile attempts of my timid adversaries have hitherto proved abortive—so far I have borne down all opposition, and those (even some of the greatest of them) who not long since were my most open, as well as secret enemies, I now behold with the most princely pleasure, the earliest to attend, to congratulate me on my birthday, tho' uninvited, bow down, and make the most submissive congees. Have you not seen this, Mocklaw? and how I keep them in expectation of something, by now and then bestowing part of a gracious smile amongst a dozen of them?

MOCKLAW. I have, my Lord, and no doubt they interpret that as a favourable omen;—however, policy, my Lord, would dictate that to you, if there were no other consideration.

PARAMOUNT. True, and yet they are cursedly mistaken—and now, Mocklaw, as I have ever found you to be well dispos'd towards me, and the cause I espouse, and as I trust you continue satisfy'd with my former bounty, and my promise now of granting you a pension for life, with liberty to retire, I shall make you my confident, and disclose to you a secret no man except myself yet knows, which I expect you have so much honour to let it remain a secret to all the world (I mean as to the main point I have in view).

MOCKLAW. Depend upon it, my Lord, I am sincerely devoted to your Lordship, command me, I care not what it is, I'll screw, twist and strain the law as tight as a drumhead, to serve you.

PARAMOUNT. I shall at this time but just give you a hint of the plan I've drawn up in my own mind. You must have perceived in me a secret hankering for majesty for some time past, notwithstanding my age;—but as I have considered the great dislike the nation in general have, as to my person, I'll wave my own pretensions, and bend my power and assiduity to it in favour of one, the nearest a kin to me, you know who I mean, and a particular friend of yours, provided I continue to be dictator,[Pg 294] as at present; and further, I intend America shall submit. What think you of it so far?

MOCKLAW. A day I've long wish'd to see! but you stagger me, my Lord, not as to my honour, secrecy, or resolution to serve you, but as to the accomplishment of such grand designs.

PARAMOUNT. 'Tis true, I have undertaken a mighty task, a task that would have perplexed the Council of Nice, and stagger'd even Julius Cæsar—but—

MOCKLAW. You have need, my Lord, of all your wisdom, fortitude and power, when you consider with whom you have to contend—Let me see—Lord Wisdom—Lord Religion—Lord Justice—Lord Patriot—the bold Irishman, &c., &c., &c., and the wisdom of the United Colonies of America in Congress to cope with; as individuals they are trifling, but in league combined may become potent enemies.

PARAMOUNT. Granted—But are you so little of a lawyer as not to know the virtue of a certain specific I'm possess'd of, that will accomplish any thing, even to performing miracles? Don't you know there's such sweet music in the shaking of the treasury keys, that they will instantly lock the most babbling patriot's tongue? transform a Tory into a Whig, and a Whig into a Tory? make a superannuated old miser dance, and an old Cynic philosopher smile. How many thousand times has your tongue danc'd at Westminster Hall to the sound of such music?

MOCKLAW. Enchanting sounds, powerful magic, there's no withstanding the charms of such music, their potency and influence are irresistible—that is a point of law I can by no means give up, of more force than all the acts of parliament since the days of King Alfred.

PARAMOUNT. I'm glad you acknowledge that—Now then for a line of politics—I propose to begin first by taxing America, as a blind—that will create an eternal animosity between us, and by sending over continually ships and troops, this will, of course, produce a civil war—weaken

Britain by leaving her coasts defenseless, and impoverish America; so that we need not fear any thing from that quarter. Then the united fleets of France and Spain with troops to appear in the channel, and make a descent, while my kinsman with thirty thousand men lands in Scotland, marches to London, and joins the others: What then can prevent the scheme from having the wish'd for effect? This is the main point, which keep to yourself.[Pg 295]

MOCKLAW. If it has failed heretofore, 'tis impossible it should fail now; nothing within the reach of human wisdom was ever planned so judiciously; had Solomon been alive, and a politician, I would have sworn your Lordship had consulted him.—But I would beg leave to hint to your Lordship the opposition to be apprehended from the militia of England, and the German forces that may be sent for according to treaty.

PARAMOUNT. As to the militia, they are half of them my friends, witness Lancaster, Manchester, Liverpool, &c., &c., &c., the other half scarce ever fired a gun in their lives, especially those of London; and I shall take care by shaking of the keys a little to have such officers appointed over them, who are well known to be in my interest. As to the German forces, I have nothing to apprehend from them; the parliament can soon pass an act against the introduction of foreign troops, except the French or Spaniards, who can't be called foreign, they are our friends and nearest neighbours. Have you any thing further to object against the probability of this plan?

MOCKLAW. Nothing, my Lord, but the people of Ireland, who must be cajoled or humbugg'd.

PARAMOUNT. As to that, let me alone, I shall grant the Roman Catholics, who are by far the most numerous, the free exercise of their religion, with the liberty of bearing arms, so long unjustly deprived of, and disarm in due time all the Protestants in their turn.

MOCKLAW. That will be a noble stroke, the more I consider it, the more I'm surpris'd at your Lordship's profound wisdom and foresight: I think success is certain.

PARAMOUNT. Then this is the favourable crisis to attempt it; 'tis not the thought of a day, a month, or a year. Have you any more objections?

MOCKLAW. I have one more, my Lord—

PARAMOUNT. Well, pray let's hear it; these lawyers will be heard.

MOCKLAW. The Bishops and Clergy are a powerful, numerous body; it would be necessary, my Lord, to gain them over, or keep them silent—A religious war is the worst of wars.

PARAMOUNT. You are very right, I have 'em fast enough—Mammon will work powerfully on them—The keys—the keys—His Grace my Lord of Suffolk is managing this business for me, and feeding them with the hopes of being all created Archbishops[Pg 296] here, and each to have a diocese, and Bishops of their own appointment in America; not a city or town there but must be provided with a Bishop: There let religion erect her holy altars, by which means their revenues will be augmented beyond that of a Cardinal. All this we must make 'em believe.

MOCKLAW. True, my Lord, what is a Bishop without faith? This is the grandest stroke of religious circumvention that ever was struck.—I've done, my Lord.

PARAMOUNT. Very well, you'll not fail to meet the privy council here this evening; in the mean time you'll go and search the statutes for other precedents to strengthen the cause; and remember I have enjoin'd you to secrecy.

MOCKLAW. Depend upon it, my Lord, I cannot prove ungrateful to your Lordship, nor such an enemy to myself.

[*Exit* MOCKLAW.

SCENE III. LORD PARAMOUNT [*solus*].

This Mocklaw is a cursed knowing dog, and I believe the father of Brazen; how readily he found an old act of parliament to my purpose, as soon as I told him I would make it worth his study; and the thoughts of a pension will make him search his old worm-eaten statute books from the reign of King Arthur down to this present time; how he raises objections too to make me think his mind is ever bent on study to serve me. The shaking of the treasury keys is a fine bait. [*Rings the bell.*] Charters, magna chartas, bill of rights, acts of assembly, resolves of congresses, trials by juries (and acts of parliament too) when they make against us, must all be annihilated; a suspending power I approve of, and of royal proclamations.

[*Enter* CHARLEY.

CHARLEY. I wait your Lordship's orders.

PARAMOUNT. Write a number of cards, and see that the Lords of the privy council, and Mr. Judas, be summoned to give their attendance this evening at six o'clock, at my Pandemonium.

CHARLEY. I'm gone, my Lord.

[*Exit* CHARLEY.

PARAMOUNT [*solus*].

How do we shew our authority? how do we maintain the royal prerogative? keep in awe the knowing ones of the opposite party, and blind the eyes of the ignorant multitude in Britain? Why, by spirited measures, by an accumulation of power, of[Pg 297] deception, and the shaking of the keys, we may hope to succeed, should that fail, I'll enforce them with the pointed bayonet; the Americans from one end to the other shall submit, in spite of all opposition; I'll listen to no overtures of reconciliation from any petty self-constituted congress, they shall submit implicitly to such terms as I of my royal indulgence please to grant. I'll shew them the impudence and weakness of their resolves, and the strength of mine; I will never soften; my inflexibility shall stand firm, and convince them the second Pharaoh is at least equal to the first. I am unalterably determined at every hazard and at the risk of every consequence to compel the colonies to absolute submission. I'll draw in treasure from every quarter, and, Solomon-like, wallow in riches; and Scotland, my dear Scotland, shall be the paradise of the world. Rejoice in the name of Paramount, and the sound of a bawbee shall be no more heard in the land of my nativity.—

SCENE IV.
Enter CHARLEY *in haste.*

CHARLEY. My Lord, the notices are all served.

PARAMOUNT. It's very well, Charley.

CHARLEY. My Lord, be pleased to turn your eyes, and look out of the window, and see the Lord Mayor, Aldermen, Common Council and Liverymen going to St. James's with the address.

PARAMOUNT. Where? Sure enough—Curse their impudence; how that squinting scoundrel swells with importance—Mind, Charley, how fond he is of bowing to the gaping multitude, and ev'ry upstart he sees at a window—I hope he'll not turn his blear eyes t'wards me—I want none of his bows, not I—Stand before me, Charley—

CHARLEY. I will, my Lord, and if he looks this way, I'll give him such a devilish grin as best suits such fellows as him, and make him remember it as long as he lives.

PARAMOUNT. Do so, Charley; I hate the dog mortally, I religiously hate him, and hope ere long to have satisfaction for his insolence and the freedoms he has taken with me and my connections: I shall never forget the many scandalous verses, lampoons and pasquinades he made upon us.

CHARLEY. Indeed, he has used your Lordship too ill ever to be forgotten or forgiven.[Pg 298]

PARAMOUNT. Damn him, I never intend to do either—See again how he bows—there again—how the mob throw up their hats, split their throats; how they huzza too; they make a mere god of the fellow; how they idolize him—Ignorant brutes!

CHARLEY. A scoundrel; he has climb'd up the stilts of preferment strangely, my Lord.

5

PARAMOUNT. Strangely, indeed; but it's our own faults.

CHARLEY. He has had better luck than honester folks; I'm surpris'd to think he has ever rose to the honour of presenting a remonstrance, or rather, that he could ever have the impudence to think of remonstrating.

PARAMOUNT. Aye, Charley, you see how unaccountably things turn out; his audacity is unparalleled—a Newgate dog.

CHARLEY. My Lord, I believe the fellow was never known to blush; and, indeed, it's an observation I made some time ago, and I believe a just one, without an exception, that those who squint never blush.

PARAMOUNT. You must be mistaken, Charley.

CHARLEY. No, my Lord, it's a fact, I had an uncle squinted exactly like him, who was guilty of many scandalous things, and yet all the parish, with the parson at their head, could not make him blush, so that at last he became a by-word—Here comes old shame-the-devil; this dog is the very spawn of him.

PARAMOUNT. Hoot, mon, ye give your uncle a shocking character.

CHARLEY. I only mention it, my Lord, for the similarity's sake.

PARAMOUNT. For the spawn of him, and the similarity's sake, I'm apt to think you've been abusing your own cousin all this while.

CHARLEY. God forbid, my Lord, I should be any how allied to him.

PARAMOUNT. I fancy, Charley, if the truth was known, your uncle did not mention you in his will, and forgot to leave you the mansion-house and farm at Gallows-hill. Am I right, Charley?

CHARLEY. You're right, my Lord, upon my honour—but—

PARAMOUNT. I thought so—Well, never mind—Ha, ha, ha, who are those two fat fellows there, that go in such state?

CHARLEY. I suppose them to be a couple of Livery Tallow-chandlers, my Lord, by their big bellies.[Pg 299]

PARAMOUNT. Ha, ha,—what work the guards would make amongst them—but they must not be called yet.—And who are those other two behind 'em?

CHARLEY. This is Mr. Hone, and the other Mr. Strap, a couple of the Corporation Barbers, forsooth.

PARAMOUNT. Ha, ha, ha, I thought they had been a couple of Dukes;—and that one—who is he with the monstrous wig?

CHARLEY. That is Mr. Alderman Pipeshank, in Newgate-street.

PARAMOUNT. A parcel of Newgate dogs altogether—Well it is a good deal of satisfaction to me to think how this fellow will be received at St. James's; he'll not return back so pleas'd as he seems to be now, I warrant you—I have taken care he shall meet with a d——d cold reception there; he will have to make his appearance before Lord Frostyface, Lord Scarecrow, Lord Sneerwell, Lord Firebrand, Lord Mawmouth, Lord Waggonjaws, Lord Gripe, Lord Brass, Lord Surly and Lord Tribulation, as hard-fac'd fellows as himself; and the beauty of it is, not one of them loves him a whit more than I do.

CHARLEY. That will be rare diversion for them that are present; he'll look then, my Lord, like Sampson making sport for the Philistines.

PARAMOUNT. Aye, but I wish he was as blind too, as Sampson was.—Well Charley, we have been dispos'd to be a little merry with this ridiculous parade, this high life below stairs. I wish you had begun your description a little sooner, before they were all gone; the looks of these wiseacres afford us some mirth, tho' we despise them and their politics, and it's not unlikely it may end in blood—Be it so, I'm prepar'd for the worst.

CHARLEY. Rather so, my Lord, than submit to such rascals.

PARAMOUNT. I'll give up my life first for a sacrifice.

[*Exit* CHARLEY.

SCENE V.

Enter MOCKLAW, POLTRON, HYPOCRITE, CATSPAW, BRAZEN, JUDAS. [*All seated.*]

PARAMOUNT. My Lords and Gentlemen, it seems opposition to our measures are making hasty strides; the discontented faction, the supporters and encouragers of rebellion, and whole hearts are tainted therewith, seem bent, if possible, on the destruction of Britain, and their own aggrandisement. Are not the daily papers filled with treasonable resolves of American[Pg 300] congresses and committees, extracts of letters, and other infamous pieces and scurrilous pamphlets, circulating with unusual industry throughout the kingdom, by the enemies of Britain, thereby poisoning the minds of our liege subjects with their detestable tenets?—And did you not this day see the procession, and that vile miscreant Lord Patriot at their head, going to St. James's with their remonstrance, in such state and parade as manifestly tended to provoke, challenge and defy majesty itself, and the powers of government? and yet nothing done to stop their pernicious effects.—Surely, my Lords and Gentlemen, you must agree with me, that it is now become highly expedient that an immediate stop should be put to such unwarrantable and dangerous proceedings, by the most vigorous and coercive measures.

MOCKLAW. I entirely agree with your Lordship, and was ever firmly of opinion, that licentiousness of every kind (particularly that of the Press) is dangerous to the state; the rabble should be kept in awe by examples of severity, and a proper respect should be enforced to superiors. I have sufficiently shewn my dislike to the freedom of the Press, by the examples I have frequently made (tho' too favourable) of several Printers, and others, who had greatly trespassed, and if they still persist, other measures should be taken with them, which the laws will point out; and as to Lord Patriot, he's a fellow that has been outlaw'd, scandal-proof, little to be got by meddling with him; I would advise to let him alone for the present, and humble America first.

MR. BRAZEN. I am very clear in it, please your Lordship; there are numbers of men in this country who are ever studying how to perplex and entangle the state, constantly thwarting government, in ev'ry laudable undertaking; this clamorous faction must be curbed, must be subdued and crush'd—our thunder must go forth, America must be conquered. I am for blood and fire to crush the rising glories of America—They boast of her strength; she must be conquered, if half of Germany is called to our assistance.

MR. POLTRON. I entirely agree with you, Mr. Brazen; my advice is, that Lord Boston and Admiral Tombstone be immediately despatch'd to Boston, with two or three regiments (tho' one would be more than sufficient) and a few ships to shut up their ports, disannul their charter, stop their trade, and the pusillanimous beggars, those scoundrel rascals, whose predomi[Pg 301]nant passion is fear, would immediately give up, on the first landing of the regulars, and fly before 'em like a hare before the hounds; that this would be the case, I pawn my honour to your Lordships, nay, I'll sacrifice my life: My Lords, I have moreover the testimony of General Amherst and Colonel Grant to back my assertion; besides, here's Mr. Judas, let him speak.

LORD HYPOCRITE. If this is the same Colonel Grant that was at Fort Duquesne, the same that ran away from the French and Indians, the same that was rescued by Colonel Washington, I have no idea of his honour or testimony.

LORD POLTRON. He's a Gentleman, my Lord Hypocrite, of undoubted veracity.

LORD HYPOCRITE. You might as well have said courage too, I have exceptions against both; and as to General Amherst's assertion that he could drive all America with five thousand men, he must have been joking, as he is quite of a diff'rent opinion now.

LORD CATSPAW. What is your opinion of your countrymen, Mr. Judas, with respect to their courage?

JUDAS. The same that I have ever told you, my Lord; as to true courage they have none, I know 'em well—they have a plenty of a kind of enthusiastic zeal, which they substitute in the room of it; I am very certain they would never face the regulars, tho' with the advantage of ten to one.

LORD HYPOCRITE. All this, and a great deal more, would never convince me of the general cowardice of the Americans—but of the cowardice of Grant I've been long convinced, by numbers of letters formerly from America—I'm for doing the business effectually; don't let us be too sanguine, trust to stories told by every sycophant, and hurry heels over head to be laugh'd at; the Americans are bold, stubborn, and sour; it will require foreign assistance to subdue 'em.

LORD CATSPAW. These four Americans, ignorant brutes, unbroke and wild, must be tamed; they'll soon be humble if punish'd; but if disregarded, grow fierce.—Barbarous nations must be held by fear, rein'd and spurr'd hard, chain'd to the oar, and bow'd to due control, till they look grim with blood; let's first humble America, and bring them under our feet; the olive-branch has been held out, and they have rejected it; it now becomes us to use the iron rod to break their disobedience; and should we lack it, foreign assistance is at hand.[Pg 302]

LORD HYPOCRITE. All this I grant, but I'm for sending a force sufficient to crush 'em at once, and not with too much precipitation; I am first for giving it a colour of impartiality, forbearance and religion.—Lay it before parliament; we have then law on our side, and endeavour to gain over some or all of the Methodist Teachers, and in particular my very good friend Mr. Wesley, their Bishop, and the worthy Mr. Clapum, which task I would undertake; it will then have the sanction of religion, make it less suspected, and give it a better grace.

LORD CATSPAW. I should choose it to be done by consent of parliament; we stand then on firmer ground; there's no doubt they'll grant ev'ry thing your Lordship proposes upon my motion: but to tell the truth, I'd rather be in Purgatory so long, than to run the gauntlet of the Bold Irishman's tongue.

MOCKLAW. Aye, aye, don't part with the law while it's in our favour, or we can have it by asking for—and as to the Bold Irishman, don't be brow-beaten, you must summon all your brass, and put on a rugged highwayman's face like his; I expect some work of that kind too, but the devil himself sha'n't browbeat me.

PARAMOUNT. I am glad to find, my Lords and Gentlemen, you all see the necessity of sending over troops and ships; I intend my Lord Catspaw shall lay it before parliament, and am very certain they'll pass any acts I can desire. I thank you, Lord Hypocrite, for your kind offer, and accept of it; my Lord of Suffolk is negotiating the same business with the rest of my Lords the Bishops, and will succeed; so that it will carry the appearance of law, of religion, and will be sufficiently grac'd; I'll warrant you no one shall have cause to complain of its wanting grace. And now, my Lords and Gentlemen, as it's so late, and we have gone through all the business at this time proposed, you are at your liberty to withdraw.

[*Exeunt.*

PARAMOUNT [*solus*].

The fate of England and America is now fixed, irrevocably fixed; the storm is ready to burst; the low'ring clouds portend their fate my glory, their fall my triumph—But I must haste to be gone, the ceremonies await my presence; deeds of darkness must be done by night, and, like the silent mole's work, under ground:

Now rushing forth in sober twilight gray,Like prowling wolf, who ranges for his prey.

[*Exit.*

[Pg 303]

ACT II.
SCENE I.
LORD WISDOM, LORD RELIGION, LORD JUSTICE.
LORD WISDOM.

I much lament, my Lords, the present unhappy situation of my country; where e'er I turn mine eyes, to Europe, Asia, Africa, or America, the prospect appears the same—Look up to the throne, and behold your king, if I may now call him by that soft title—Where is the wisdom, the justice, the religion, that once adorn'd that throne, and shed the benign influence of their bright rays thro' the four quarters of the globe? Alas! they're flown!

Mark his forlorn looks—his countenance dejected, a sullen greatness fixed on his brow, as if it veil'd in blood some awful purpose, his eyes flaming and sanguinary; how I bewail you, for your predecessor's sake! Long, long have I been an old, and I trust a faithful, servant in the family—Can I then restrain one tear? No, 'tis impossible! View that arch-dragon, that old fiend, Paramount, that rebel in grain, whispering in his ear. View his wretched ministers hovering round him, to accomplish their accursed purpose, and accelerate his destruction. View the whole herd of administration (I know 'em well) and tell me if the world can furnish a viler set of miscreants? View both houses of parliament, and count the number of Tyrants, Jacobites, Tories, Placemen, Pensioners, Sycophants, and Panders. View the constitution, is she not disrob'd and dismantled? is she not become like a virgin deflower'd? View our fleets and armies commanded by bloody, murdering butchers! View Britain herself as a sheep without a shepherd! And lastly view America, for her virtue bleeding and for her liberty weltering in her blood!

LORD RELIGION. Such hath, and ever will be the fate of kings, who only listen to the voice of pleasure, thrown in their way by the sirens of administration, which never fail to swallow them up like quicksand—like a serpent, who charms and fascinates, bewitches and enchants with his eye the unwary bird; witness the fatal catastrophe of Rehoboam, who rejected the counsel of the wise and experienced, and gave up all to the advice and guidance of young, unskilful and wicked counsellors. Had he listen'd to you, my Lord, had he followed your advice, all, all would have gone well— Under your auspicious adminis[Pg 304]tration Britain flourished, but ever since has been on the decline and patriotism, like religion, scarcely now more than a sounding brass or a tinkling cymbal.

LORD WISDOM. My counsel has been rejected—my conciliatory plan thrown under the table, and treated with contempt; the experience of gray hairs called the superannuated notions of old age—my bodily infirmities—my tottering frame—my crazy carcase, worn out in the service of my country, and even my very crutches, have been made the subject of their ridicule.

LORD JUSTICE. Gratitude, like religion and patriotism, are about taking their flight, and the law of the land stands on tip-toe; the constitution, that admirable fabric, that work of ages, the envy of the world, is deflower'd indeed, and made to commit a rape upon her own body, by the avaricious frowns of her own father, who is bound to protect her, not to destroy.—Her pillars are thrown down, her capitals broke, her pedestals demolish'd, and her foundation nearly destroy'd.—Lord Paramount and his wretched adviser Mocklaw baffle all our efforts.—The statutes of the land superseded by royal proclamations and dispensing powers, &c., &c., the bloody knife to be held to the throats of the Americans, and force them to submit to slav'ry.—Administration have commenced bloody tyrants, and those that should protect the subject are become their executioners; yet will I dispute with them inch by inch, while there's a statute book left in the land. Come forth, thou grand deceiver! I challenge thee to come forth!

LORD WISDOM. Our friends must bestir themselves once more, perhaps we may yet turn the scale.—If the voice of religion, wisdom and justice should fail, let us sound the trumpet of liberty and patriotism, that will conquer them in America, I know; let us try to storm them here with the united whole, and if by a base majority they still carry their point, we can nevertheless wash our hands and be clean.

LORD RELIGION. From the pulpit, in the house of God, have I spoken aloud, I have lifted up my voice like a trumpet. O Britain, how art thou fallen! Hear now, O house of Britain, is it a small thing for you to weary man, but will you weary your God also? In the house of Lords have I borne my testimony: Hear now, O ye Princes, and I will yet declare in Britain, and shew forth in America, I will not cease till I bring about (if possible) unity, peace and concord.[Pg 305]

LORD WISDOM. Much to be wished for; but alas! I fear it's now too late; I foresee the tendency and consequence of those diabolical measures that have been pursued with unrelenting fury. Britain will ruin her trade, waste her wealth, her strength, her credit and her importance in the scale of Europe. When a British king proves ungrateful and haughty, and strives to be independent of his people (who are his sole support), the people will in their turn likewise strive to be independent of him and his myrmidons, and will be free; they will erect the anfractuous standard of independency, and thousands and tens of thousands will flock to it, and solace themselves under its shade.—They has often been told of this, but affected to despise it; they know not America's strength, they are ignorant of it; fed by the flatt'ry of every sycophant tale, imagine themselves almighty, and able to subdue the whole world. America will be lost to Britain forever, and will prove her downfall. America is wise, and will shake off the galling yoke before it be rivetted on them; they will be drove to it, and who can blame them? Who can blame a galley-slave for making his escape?—Britain will miscarry in her vile projects, her knight errant, her Don Quixote schemes in America: America will resist; they are not easily to be subdued (nay, 'tis impossible); Britain will find it a harder task than to conquer France and Spain united, and will cost 'em more blood and treasure than a twice Seven Years' War with those European powers; they will stand out till Britons are tired. Britain will invite her with kind promises and open arms; America will reject them; America will triumph, rejoice and flourish, and become the glory of the earth; Britain will languidly hold down her head, and become first a prey to a vile Pretender, and then be subject to the ravagers of Europe. I love the Americans, because they love liberty. Liberty flourishes in the wilds of America. I honour the plant, I revere the tree, and would cherish its branches. Let us, my friends, join hands with them, follow their example, and endeavour to support expiring liberty in Britain; whilst I have a tongue to speak, I will support her wherever found; while I have crutches to crawl with, I will try to find her out, and with the voice of an archangel will demand for a sacrifice to the nation those miscreants who have wickedly and wantonly been the ruin of their country. O Liberty! O my Country!

LORD RELIGION. O Religion! O Virtue! whither art thou fleeing? O thou Defender of the Faith? O ye mighty Lords[Pg 306] and Commons! O ye deluded Bishops, ye learned props of our unerring church, who preach up vengeance, force and fire, instead of peace! be wise in time, lest the Americans be driven to work out their own salvation without fear or trembling.

[Exeunt.

SCENE II.
LORD PATRIOT, BOLD IRISHMAN, COLONEL.
BOLD IRISHMAN.

That Brazen Lawyer,[7] that Lord Chancellor, that wou'd be, held forth surprisingly last night, he beat the drum in your ears, brother soldier.

COLONEL. I think he did; he beat a Tatoo for us all.

LORD PATRIOT. No politicians, but lawyer politicians, it seems will go down; if we believe him, we must all turn lawyers now, and prate away the liberties of the nation.

COLONEL. Aye, first we must learn to rail at the clamourous faction, disappointed politicians—ever restless—ever plotting—constantly thwarting government, in laudable and blameable purposes.—Inconsiderable party—inconsistent in their own politics—hostile to all government, soured by disappointment, and urged by want—proceeding to unjustifiable lengths—and then sound the magnanimity of a British senate, animated by the sacred fire caught from a high-spirited people—

BOLD IRISHMAN. And the devil knows what beside—Magnanimity and sacred fire, indeed!—Very magnanimous sounds, but pompous nothings! Why did he not tell us where was the magnanimity of the British senate at the time of the dispute about Falkland's Island? What sort of fire animated them then?—Where was the high spirit of the people?—Strange sort of fire, and strange sort of spirit, to give up to our inveterate enemies, the Spaniards, our property unasked for, and cut our best friends and brethren, the Americans' throats, for defending theirs against lawless tyranny; their sacred fire became then all fume, and the strength of their boasted spirits evaporated into invisible effluvium; the giant then sunk sure enough spontaneously into a dwarf; and now, it seems, the dwarf having been feeding upon smoky fire and evaporated spirits, is endeavouring to swell himself into a giant again, like the frog in the fable, till he bursts himself in silent thunder—But let the mighty Philistine, the Goliath Paramount, and his oracle Mocklaw,[Pg 307] with their thunder bellowed from the brazen mortar-piece of a turn-coat lawyer, have a care of the little American David!

LORD PATRIOT. Aye, indeed! America will prove a second Sampson to 'em; they may put out his eyes for a while, but he'll pull their house down about their ears for all that. Mr. Brazen seem'd surpris'd at the thought of relinquishing America, and bawl'd out with the vociferation of an old miser that had been robb'd—Relinquish America! relinquish America! forbid it heavens! But let him and his masters take great care, or America will save 'em the trouble, and relinquish Britain.

COLONEL. Or I'm much mistaken, Brazen says, establish first your superiority, and then talk of negotiating.

LORD PATRIOT. That doctrine suits 'em best; just like a cowardly pickpocket, or a bloody highwayman, knock a man down first, and then tell him stand and deliver.

COLONEL. A just comparison, and excellent simile, by my soul! But I'm surpris'd he did not include the Clergy among the number of professions unfit (as he said) to be politicians.

BOLD IRISHMAN. Did you ever know a lawyer to be concerned with religion, unless he got a fee by it? he'll take care and steer clear of that; if it don't come in his way, he'll never break his neck over a church bible, I warrant you—Mammon is his god—Judge Jeffereys is his priest—Star-chamber doctrine is his creed—fire, flames and faggot, blood, murder, halters and thund'ring cannon are the ceremonies of his church—and lies, misrepresentations, deceit, hypocrisy and dissimulation are the articles of his religion.

LORD PATRIOT. You make him a monster, indeed.

BOLD IRISHMAN. Not half so bad as he is, my Lord; he's following close to the heels of that profound sage, that oracle, Mocklaw, his tutor. I can compare the whole herd of them to nothing else but to the swine we read of running headlong down the hill, Paramount their devil, Mocklaw the evil spirit, and Brazen their driver.

COLONEL. And thus they'll drive liberty from out the land; but when a brave people, like the Americans, from their infancy us'd to liberty (not as a gift, but who inherit it as a birth-right, but not as a mess of pottage, to be bought by, or sold to, ev'ry hungry glutton of a minister) find attempts made to reduce them to slavery, they generally take some desperate successful measure for their deliverance. I should not be at all surpris'd to hear of[Pg 308] independency proclaim'd throughout their land, of Britain's armies beat, their fleets burnt, sunk, or otherwise destroy'd. The same principle which Mr. Brazen speaks of, that inspires British soldiers to fight, namely the ferment of youthful blood, the high spirit of the people, a love of glory, and a sense of national honour, will inspire the Americans to withstand them; to which I may add, liberty and property.—But what is national honour? Why, national pride.—What is national glory? Why, national nonsense, when put in competition with liberty and property.

LORD PATRIOT. Of Britain I fear liberty has taken its farewell, the aspiring wings of tyranny hath long hovered over, and the over-shadowing influence of bribery hath eclips'd its rays and dark'ned its lustre; the huge Paramount, that temporal deity, that golden calf, finds servile wretches enough so base as to bow down, worship and adore his gilded horns;—let 'em e'en if they will:—But as for me, tho' I should stand alone, I would spurn the brute, were he forty-five[8] times greater than he is; I'll administer, ere long, such an emetic to him, as shall make the monster disgorge the forty millions yet unaccounted for, and never shall it be said, that Patriot ever feared or truckled to him, or kept a silent tongue when it should speak.

BOLD IRISHMAN. There I'll shake hands with you, and my tongue shall echo in their ears, make their arched ceiling speak, the treasury bench crack, and the great chair of their great speaker tremble, and never will I cease lashing them, while lashing is good, or hope remains; and when

8

the voice of poor liberty can no longer be heard in Britain or Hibernia, let's give Caledonia a kick with our heels, and away with the goddess to the American shore, crown her, and defy the grim king of tyranny, at his peril, to set his foot there.—Here let him stay, and wallow in sackcloth and ashes, like a beast as he is, and, Nebuchadnezzar-like, eat grass and thistles.

[*Exeunt.*

See Paramount, upon his awful throne, Striving to make each freeman's purse his own! While Lords and Commons most as one agree, To grace his head with crown of tyranny. They spurn the laws,—force constitution locks, To seize each subject's coffer, chest and box;, Send justice packing, as tho' too pure unmix'd, And hug the tyrant, as if by law he's fix'd.

FOOTNOTES:

[7]See Wedderburne's Speech.
[8]Alluding to North-Briton, Number forty-five.

[Pg 309]

ACT III.
Scene I. *In Boston.*
SELECTMAN, CITIZEN.
SELECTMAN.

At length, it seems, the bloody flag is hung out, the ministry and parliament, ever studious in mischief, and bent on our destruction, have ordered troops and ships of war to shut our ports, and starve us into submission.

CITIZEN. And compel us to be slaves; I have heard so. It is a fashionable way to requite us for our loyalty, for the present we made them of Louisburg, for our protection at Duquesne, for the assistance we gave them at Quebec, Martinico, Guadaloupe and the Havannah. Blast their councils, spurn their ingratitude! Soul of Pepperel! whither art thou fled?

SELECTMAN. They seem to be guided by some secret demon; this stopping our ports and depriving us of all trade is cruel, calculated to starve and beggar thousands of families, more spiteful than politic, more to their own disadvantage than ours: But we can resolve to do without trade; it will be the means of banishing luxury, which has ting'd the simplicity and spotless innocence of our once happy asylum.

CITIZEN. We thank heaven, we have the necessaries of life in abundance, even to an exuberant plenty; and how oft have our hospitable tables fed numbers of those ungrateful monsters, who would now, if they could, famish us?

SELECTMAN. No doubt, as we abound in those temporal blessings, it has tempted them to pick our pockets by violence, in hopes of treasures more to their minds.

CITIZEN. In that these thirsters after gold and human blood will be disappointed. No Perus or Mexicos here they'll find; but the demon you speak of, tho' he acts in secret, is notoriously known. Lord Paramount is that demon, that bird of prey, that ministerial cormorant, that waits to devour, and who first thought to disturb the repose of America; a wretch, no friend to mankind, who acts thro' envy and avarice, like Satan, who 'scap'd from hell to disturb the regions of paradise; after ransacking Britain and Hibernia for gold, the growth of hell, to feed his luxury, now waits to rifle the bowels of America.

SELECTMAN. May he prove more unsuccessful than Satan; blind politics, rank infatuation, madness detestable, the con[Pg 310]comitants of arbitrary power! They can never think to succeed; but should they conquer, they'll find that he who overcometh by force and blood, hath overcome but half his foe. Capt. Preston's massacre is too recent in our memories; and if a few troops dar'd to commit such hellish unprovok'd barbarities, what may we not expect from legions arm'd with vengeance, whose leaders harbour principles repugnant to freedom, and possess'd with more than diabolical notions? Surely our friends will oppose them with all the power heaven has given them.

CITIZEN. Nothing more certain; each citizen and each individual inhabitant of America are bound by the ties of nature; the laws of God and man justify such a procedure; passive obedience for passive slaves, and non-resistance for servile wretches who know not, neither deserve, the sweets of liberty. As for me and my house, thank God, such detestable doctrine never did, nor ever shall, enter over my threshold.

SELECTMAN. Would all America were so zealous as you.—The appointment of a general Continental Congress was a judicious measure, and will prove the salvation of this new world, where counsel mature, wisdom and strength united; it will prove a barrier, a bulwark, against the encroachments of arbitrary power.

CITIZEN. I much approve of the choice of a congress; America is young, she will be to it like a tender nursing mother, she will give it the paps of virtue to suck, cherish it with the milk of liberty, and fatten it on the cream of patriotism; she will train it up in its youth, and teach it to shun the poison of British voluptuousness, and instruct it to keep better company. Let us, my friend, support her all in our power, and set on foot an immediate association; they will form an intrenchment, too strong for ministerial tyranny to o'erleap.

SELECTMAN. I am determined so to do, it may prevent the farther effusion of blood.

Scene II.
Enter a MINISTER.
MINISTER.

My friends, I yet will hail you good morrow, tho' I know not how long we may be indulg'd that liberty to each other; doleful tidings I have to tell.[Pg 311]

SELECTMAN. With sorrow we have heard it, good morrow, sir.

MINISTER. Wou'd to God it may prove false, and that it may vanish like the dew of the morning.

CITIZEN. Beyond a doubt, sir, it's too true.

MINISTER. Perhaps, my friends, you have not heard all.

SELECTMAN. We have heard too much, of the troops and ships coming over, we suppose you mean; we have not heard more, if more there be.

MINISTER. Then worse I have to tell, tidings which will raise the blood of the patriot, and put your virtue to the proof, will kindle such an ardent love of liberty in your breasts, as time will not be able to exterminate—

CITIZEN. Pray, let us hear it, I'm all on fire.

SELECTMAN. I'm impatient to know it, welcome or unwelcome.

MINISTER. Such as it is, take it; your charter is annihilated; you are all, all declared rebels; your estates are to be confiscated; your patrimony to be given to those who never labour'd for it; popery to be established in the room of the true catholic faith; the Old South, and other houses of our God, converted perhaps into nunneries, inquisitions, barracks and common jails, where you will perish with want and famine, or suffer an ignominious death; your wives, children, dearest relations and friends forever separated from you in this world, without the prospect of receiving any comfort or consolation from them, or the least hope of affording any to them.

SELECTMAN. Perish the thought!

CITIZEN. I've heard enough!—To arms! my dear friends, to arms! and death or freedom be our motto!

MINISTER. A noble resolution! Posterity will crown the urn of the patriot who consecrates his talents to virtue and freedom; his name shall not be forgot; his reputation shall bloom with unfading verdure, while the name of the tyrant, like his vile body, shall moulder in the dust. Put your trust in the Lord of hosts, he is your strong tower, he is your helper and defense, he will guide and strengthen the arm of flesh, and scatter your enemies like chaff.

SELECTMAN. Let us not hesitate.

CITIZEN. Not a single moment;—'tis like to prove a mortal strife, a never-ending contest.

MINISTER. Delays may be dangerous.—Go and awake your brethren that sleep;—rouse them up from their lethargy and[Pg 312] supineness, and join, with confidence, temporal with spiritual weapons. Perhaps they be now landing, and this moment, this very moment, may be the last of your liberty. Prepare yourselves—be ready—stand fast—ye know not the day nor the hour. May the Ruler of all send us liberty and life. Adieu! my friends.

[*Exeunt.*

SCENE III. *In a street in Boston.*

*Frequent town-meetings and consultations amongst the inhabitants;—*LORD BOSTON *arrives with the forces and ships;—lands and fortifies Boston.*

WHIG *and* TORY.

WHIG. I have said and done all that man could say or do.—'Tis wrong, I insist upon it, and time will show it, to suffer them to take possession of Castle William and fortify Boston Neck.

TORY. I cannot see, good sir, of what advantage it will be to them;—they've only a mind, I suppose, to keep their soldiers from being inactive, which may prejudice their health.

WHIG. I wish it may prove so, I would very gladly confess your superior knowledge in military manœuvres; but till then, suffer me to tell you, it's a stroke the most fatal to us,—no less, sir, but to cut off the communication between the town and country, making prisoners of us all by degrees, and give 'em an opportunity of making excursions, and in a short time subdue us without resistance.

TORY. I think your fears are groundless.

WHIG. Sir, my reason is not to be trifled with. Do you not see or hear ev'ry day of insults and provocations to the peaceable inhabitants? This is only a prelude. Can men of spirit bear forever with such usage? I know not what business they have here at all.

TORY. I suppose they're come to protect us.

WHIG. Damn such protectors, such cut-throat villains; protect us? from what? from whom?—

TORY. Nay, sir, I know not their business;—let us yet bear with them till we know the success of the petition from the Congress;—if unfavourable, then it will be our time.

WHIG. Then, I fear, it will be too late; all that time we lose, and they gain ground; I have no notion of trusting to the success of petitions, waiting twelve months for no answer at all. Our[Pg 313] assemblies have petitioned often, and as often in vain; 't would be a miracle in these days to hear of an American petition being granted; their omnipotences, their demi-godships (as they think themselves) no doubt think it too great a favour done us to throw our petitions under their table, much less vouchsafe to read them.

TORY. You go too far;—the power of King, Lords and Commons is uncontroulable.

WHIG. With respect to tyrannising they would make it so, if they could, I know, but there's a good deal to be said and done first; we have more than half the bargain to make.

TORY. Sure you would not go to dispute by arms with Great-Britain.

WHIG. Sure I would not suffer you to pick my pocket, sir.

TORY. If I did, the law is open for you—

WHIG. I have but a poor opinion of law, when the devil sits judge.

TORY. What would you do then, sir, if I was to pick your pocket?

WHIG. Break your head, sir—

TORY. Sure you don't mean as you say, sir—

WHIG. I surely do—try me, sir—

TORY. Excuse me, sir, I am not of your mind, I would avoid every thing that has the appearance of rashness.—Great-Britain's power, sir—

WHIG. Great-Britain's power, sir, is too much magnified, 't will soon grow weak, by endeavouring to make slaves of American freemen; we are not Africans yet, neither bond-slaves.—You would avoid and discourage every thing that has the appearance of patriotism, you mean.—

TORY. Who? me, sir?

WHIG. Yes, you, sir;—you go slyly pimping, spying and sneaking about, cajoling the ignorant, and insinuating bugbear notions of Great-Britain's mighty power into weak people's ears, that we may tamely give all up, and you be rewarded, perhaps, with the office of judge of the admiralty, or continental hangman, for ought I know.

TORY. Who? me, sir?

WHIG. Aye, you, sir;—and let me tell you, sir, you've been long suspected—

TORY. Of what, sir?[Pg 314]

WHIG. For a rank Tory, sir.

TORY. What mean you, sir?

WHIG. I repeat it again—suspected to be an enemy to your country.

TORY. By whom, sir? Can you show me an instance?

WHIG. From your present discourse I suspect you—and from your connections and artful behaviour all suspect you.

TORY. Can you give me a proof?

WHIG. Not a point blank proof, as to my own knowledge; you're so much of a Jesuit, you have put it out of my power;—but strong circumstances by information, such as amount to a proof in the present case, sir, I can furnish you with.

TORY. Sir, you may be mistaken.

WHIG. 'Tis not possible, my informant knows you too well.

TORY. Who is your informant, sir?

WHIG. A gentleman, sir; and if you'll give yourself the trouble to walk with me, I'll soon produce him.

TORY. Another time; I cannot stay now;—'tis dinner time.

WHIG. That's the time to find him.

TORY. I cannot stay now.

WHIG. We'll call at your house then.

TORY. I dine abroad, sir.

WHIG. Be gone, you scoundrel! I'll watch your waters; 'tis time to clear the land of such infernal vermin.

[*Exeunt both different ways.*

LORD BOSTON *surrounded by his guards and a few officers.*

LORD BOSTON. If Colonel Smith succeeds in his embassy, and I think there's no doubt of it, I shall have the pleasure this ev'ning, I expect, of having my friends Hancock and Adams's good company; I'll make each of them a present of a pair of handsome iron ruffles, and Major Provost shall provide a suitable entertainment for them in his apartment.

OFFICER. Sure they'll not be so unpolite as to refuse your Excellency's kind invitation.

LORD BOSTON. Shou'd they, Colonel Smith and Major Pitcairn have my orders to make use of all their rhetoric and the persuasive eloquence of British thunder.[Pg 315]

Enter a MESSENGER *in haste.*

MESSENGER. I bring your Excellency unwelcome tidings—

LORD BOSTON. For heaven's sake! from what quarter?

MESSENGER. From Lexington plains.

LORD BOSTON. 'Tis impossible!

MESSENGER. Too true, sir.

LORD BOSTON. Say—what is it? Speak what you know.

MESSENGER. Colonel Smith is defeated, and fast retreating.

LORD BOSTON. Good God!—What does he say? Mercy on me!

MESSENGER. They're flying before the enemy.

LORD BOSTON. Britons turn their backs before the Rebels!—The Rebels put Britons to flight?—Said you not so?

MESSENGER. They are routed, sir;—they are flying this instant;—the Provincials are numerous, and hourly gaining strength;—they have nearly surrounded our troops. A reinforcement, sir—a timely succour may save the shatter'd remnant Speedily! speedily, sir! or they're irretrievably lost!

LORD BOSTON. Good God! What does he say? Can it be possible?

MESSENGER. Lose no time, sir.

LORD BOSTON. What can I do?—Oh dear!

OFFICER. Draw off a detachment—form a brigade; prepare part of the train; send for Lord Percy; let the drums beat to arms.

LORD BOSTON. Aye, do, Captain; you know how, better than I. (*Exit* OFFICER.) Did the Rebels dare to fire on the king's troops? Had they the courage? Guards, keep round me.

MESSENGER. They're like lions; they have killed many of our bravest officers and men; and if not checked instantly, will totally surround them, and make the whole prisoners. This is no time to parley, sir.

LORD BOSTON. No, indeed; what will become of me?

Enter EARL PERCY.

EARL PERCY. Your orders, sir.

LORD BOSTON. Haste, my good Percy, immediately take command of the brigade of reinforcement, and fly to the assistance of poor Smith!—Lose no time, lest they be all cut off, and the Rebels improve their advantage, and be upon us; and God knows what quarter they'll give.—Haste, my noble Earl!—Speedily!—Speedily!—Where's my guard?[Pg 316]

EARL PERCY. I'm gone, sir.

[*Exeunt* PERCY *and* OFFICERS—*drums beating to arms.*

LORD BOSTON. What means this flutt'ring round my heart? this unusual chilness? Is it fear? No, it cannot be, it must proceed from my great anxiety, my perturbation of mind for the fate of my countrymen. A drowsiness hangs o'er my eyelids;—fain would I repose myself a short time;—but I must not;—I must wait;—I'll to the top of yon eminence,—there I shall be safer. Here I cannot stay;—there I may behold something favourable to calm this tumult in my breast.—But, alas! I fear—Guards, attend me.

[*Exeunt* LORD BOSTON *and* GUARDS.

SCENE V. LORD BOSTON *and* GUARDS *on a hill in Boston, that overlooks Charlestown.*

LORD BOSTON. Clouds of dust and smoke intercept my sight; I cannot see; I hear the noise of cannon—Percy's cannon—Grant him success!

OFFICER OF GUARD. Methinks, sir, I see British colours waving.

LORD BOSTON. Some ray of hope.—Have they got so near?—Captain, keep a good lookout; tell me every thing you see. My eyes are wondrous dim.

OFFICER. The two brigades have join'd—Now Admiral Tombstone bellows his lower tier on the Provincials. How does your Excellency?

LORD BOSTON. Right;—more hope still.—I'm bravely to what I was. Which way do our forces tend?

OFFICER. I can distinguish nothing for a certainty now; such smoke and dust!

LORD BOSTON. God grant Percy courage!

OFFICER. His ancestors were brave, sir.

LORD BOSTON. Aye, that's no rule—no rule, Captain; so were mine.—A heavy firing now.—The Rebels must be very numerous—

OFFICER. They're like caterpillars; as numerous as the locusts of Egypt.

LORD BOSTON. Look out, Captain, God help you, look out.

OFFICER. I do, sir.

LORD BOSTON. What do you see now? Hark! what dreadful noise!

ONE OF THE GUARD. [*Aside.*] How damn'd afraid he is.[Pg 317]

ANOTHER OF THE GUARD. [*Aside.*] He's one of your chimney corner Generals—an old granny.

OFFICER. If I mistake not, our troops are fast retreating; their fire slackens; the noise increases.

LORD BOSTON. Oh, Captain, don't say so!

OFFICER. 'Tis true, sir, they're running—the enemy shout victory.

LORD BOSTON. Upon your honour?—say—

OFFICER. Upon my honour, sir, they're flying t'wards Charlestown. Percy's beat;—I'm afraid he's lost his artillery.

LORD BOSTON. Then 'tis all over—the day is lost—what more can we do?

OFFICER. We may, with the few troops left in Boston, yet afford them some succour, and cover their retreat across the water; 'tis impossible to do more.

LORD BOSTON. Go instantly; I'll wait your return. Try your utmost to prevent the Rebels from crossing. Success attend you, my dear Captain, God prosper you! [*Exit* OFFICER.] Alas! alas! my glory's gone; my honour's stain'd. My dear guards, don't leave me, and you shall have plenty of porter and sour-crout.

SCENE VI. ROGER *and* DICK, *two shepherds near Lexington, after the defeat and flight of the Regulars.*

ROGER. Whilst early looking, Dick, ere the sun was seen to tinge the brow of the mountain, for my flock of sheep, nor dreaming of approaching evil, suddenly mine eyes beheld from yon hill a cloud of dust arise at a small distance; the intermediate space were thick set with laurels, willows, evergreens, and bushes of various kinds, the growth of wild nature, and which hid the danger from my eyes, thinking perchance my flock had thither stray'd; I descended, and straight onward went; but, Dick, judge you my thoughts at such a disappointment: Instead of my innocent flock of sheep, I found myself almost encircled by a herd of ravenous British wolves.

DICK. Dangerous must have been your situation, Roger, whatever were your thoughts.

ROGER. I soon discovered my mistake; finding a hostile appearance, I instantly turn'd myself about, and fled to alarm the shepherds.[Pg 318]

DICK. Did they pursue you?

ROGER. They did; but having the start, and being acquainted with the by-ways, I presently got clear of their voracious jaws.

DICK. A lucky escape, indeed, Roger; and what route did they take after that?

ROGER. Onwards, t'wards Lexington, devouring geese, cattle and swine, with fury and rage, which, no doubt, was increased by their disappointment; and what may appear strange to you Dick (tho' no more strange than true), is, they seem'd to be possessed of a kind of brutish music, growling something like our favourite tune Yankee Doodle (perhaps in ridicule), till it were almost threadbare, seeming vastly pleased (monkey-like) with their mimickry, as tho' it provoked us much.

DICK. Nature, Roger, has furnish'd some brute animals with voices, or, more properly speaking, with organs of sound that nearly resemble the human. I have heard of crocodiles weeping like a child, to decoy the unwary traveller, who is no sooner within their reach, but they seize and devour instantly.

ROGER. Very true, Dick, I have read of the same; and these wolves, being of the canine breed, and having the properties of blood-hounds, no doubt are possess'd of a more acute sense of smelling, more reason, instinct, sagacity, or what shall I call it? than all other brutes. It might have been a piece of cunning of theirs, peculiar to them, to make themselves pass for shepherds, and decoy our flocks; for, as you know, Dick, all our shepherds both play and sing Yankee Doodle, our sheep and lambs are as well acquainted with that tune as ourselves, and always make up to us whene'er they hear the sound.

DICK. Yes, Roger; and now you put me in mind of it I'll tell you of something surprising in my turn: I have an old ram and an old ewe, that, whenever they sing Yankee Doodle together, a skilful musician can scarcely distinguish it from the bass and tenor of an organ.

ROGER. Surprising indeed, Dick, nor do I in the least doubt it; and why not, as well as Balaam's ass, speak? and I might add, many other asses, now-a-days; and yet, how might that music be improved by a judicious disposition of its various parts, by the addition of a proper number of sheep and young lambs; 't would then likewise resemble the counter, counter tenor, treble, and finest pipes of an organ, and might be truly called nature's organ; methinks, Dick, I could forever sit and hear such music,[Pg 319]

Where all the parts in complication roll, And with its charming music feast the soul!

DICK. Delightful, indeed; I'll attempt it with what little skill I have in music; we may then defy these wolves to imitate it, and thereby save our flocks: I am well convinced, Roger, these wolves intended it rather as a decoy than by way of ridicule, because they live by cunning and deception; besides, they could never mean to ridicule a piece of music, a tune, of which such brutes cannot be supposed to be judges, and, which is allowed by the best masters of music to be a composition of the most sublime kind, and would have done honour to a Handel or a Correllius. Well, go on, Roger, I long to hear the whole.

ROGER. When they came to Lexington, where a flock of our innocent sheep and young lambs, as usual, were feeding and sporting on the plain, these dogs of violence and rapine with haughty stride advanc'd, and berated them in a new and unheard of language to us.

DICK. I suppose learn'd at their own fam'd universities—

ROGER. No doubt; they had teachers among them—two old wolves their leaders, not unlike in features to Smith and Pitcairn, as striving to outvie each other in the very dregs of brutal eloquence, and more than Billingsgate jargon, howl'd in their ears such a peal of new-fangled execrations, and hell-invented oratory, till that day unheard in New-England, as struck the whole flock with horror, and made them for a while stand aghast, as tho' all the wolves in the forest had broke loose upon them.

DICK. Oh, shocking!—Roger, go on.

ROGER. Not content with this, their murdering leaders, with premeditated malice, keen appetite, and without provocation, gave the howl for the onset, when instantly the whole herd, as if the devil had entered into them, ran violently down the hill, and fixed their talons and jaws upon them, and as quick as lightning eight innocent young lambs fell a sacrifice to their fury, and victims to their rapacity; the very houses of our God were no longer a sanctuary; many they tore to pieces, and some at the very foot of the altar; others were dragged out as in a wanton, gamesome mood.

DICK. Barbarity inexpressible! more than savage cruelty! I hope you'll make their master pay for 'em; there is a law of this province, Roger, which obliges the owner of such dogs to pay for the mischief they do.[Pg 320]

ROGER. I know it, Dick; he shall pay, never fear, and that handsomely too; he has paid part of it already.

DICK. Who is their master, Roger?

ROGER. One Lord Paramount; they call him a free-booter; a fellow who pretends to be proprietor of all America, and says he has a deed for it, and chief ranger of all the flocks, and pretends to have a patent for it; has been a long time in the practice of killing and stealing sheep in England and Ireland, and had like to have been hang'd for it there, but was reprieved by the means of his friend *George*—I forgot his other name—not Grenville—not George the Second—but another George—

DICK. It's no matter, he'll be hang'd yet; he has sent his dogs to a wrong place, and lugg'd the wrong sow by the ear; he should have sent them to Newfoundland, or Kamchatka, there's no sheep there—But never mind, go on, Roger.

ROGER. Nor was their voracious appetites satiated there; they rush'd into the town of Concord, and proceeded to devour every thing that lay in their way; and those brute devils, like Sampson's foxes (and as tho' they were men), thrice attempted with firebrands to destroy our corn, our town-house and habitations.

DICK. Heavens! Could not all this provoke you?

ROGER. It did; rage prompted us at length, and found us arms 'gainst such hellish mischief to oppose.

DICK. Oh, would I had been there!

ROGER. Our numbers increasing, and arm'd with revenge, we in our turn play'd the man; they, unus'd to wounds, with hideous yelling soon betook themselves to a precipitate and confused flight, nor did we give o'er the chase, till Phœbus grew drowsy, bade us desist, and wished us a good night.

DICK. Of some part of their hasty retreat I was a joyful spectator, I saw their tongues lolling out of their mouths, and heard them pant like hunted wolves indeed.

ROGER. Did you not hear how their mirth was turn'd into mourning? their fury into astonishment? how soon they quitted their howling Yankee Doodle, and chang'd their notes to bellowing? how nimbly (yet against their will) they betook themselves to dancing? And he was then the bravest dog that beat time the swiftest, and footed Yankee Doodle the nimblest.

DICK. Well pleased, Roger, was I with the chase, and glorious sport it was: I oft perceiv'd them tumbling o'er each other heels[Pg 321] over head; nor did one dare stay to help his brother—but, with bloody breech, made the best of his way—nor ever stopped till they were got safe within their lurking-holes—

ROGER. From whence they have not the courage to peep out, unless four to one, except (like a skunk) forc'd by famine.

DICK. May this be the fate of all those prowling sheep-stealers, it behooves the shepherds to double the watch, to take uncommon precaution and care of their tender flocks, more especially as this is like to be an uncommon severe winter, by the appearance of wolves, so early in the season—but, hark!—Roger, methinks I hear the sound of melody warbling thro' the grove—Let's sit a while, and partake of it unseen.

ROGER. With all my heart.—Most delightful harmony! This is the First of May; our shepherds and nymphs are celebrating our glorious St. Tammany's day; we'll hear the song out, and then join in the frolic, and chorus it o'er and o'er again—This day shall be devoted to joy and festivity.

SONG.

[TUNE. *The hounds are all out, &c.*]

1.

Of *St. George*, or *St. Bute*, let the poet Laureat sing,Of *Pharaoh* or *Pluto* of old,While he rhymes forth their praise, in false, flattering lays,I'll sing of St. Tamm'ny the bold, my brave boys.

2.

Let Hibernia's sons boast, make Patrick their toast;And Scots Andrew's fame spread abroad.Potatoes and oats, and Welch leeks for Welch goats,Was never St. Tammany's food, my brave boys.

3.

In freedom's bright cause, Tamm'ny pled with applause,And reason'd most justly from nature;For this, this was his song, all, all the day long:Liberty's the right of each creature, brave boys.

4.

Whilst under an oak his great parliament sat,His throne was the crotch of the tree;With Solomon's look, without statutes or book,He wisely sent forth his decree, my brave boys.[Pg 322]

5.

His subjects stood round, not the least noise or sound,Whilst freedom blaz'd full in each face:So plain were the laws, and each pleaded his cause;That might *Bute, North* and *Mansfield* disgrace, my brave boys.

6.

No duties, nor stamps, their blest liberty cramps,A king, tho' no *tyrant*, was he;He did oft'times declare, nay, sometimes wou'd swear,The least of his subjects were free, my brave boys.

7.

He, as king of the woods, of the rivers and floods,Had a right all beasts to controul;Yet, content with a few, to give nature her due:So gen'rous was Tammany's soul! my brave boys.

8.

In the morn he arose, and a-hunting he goes,Bold Nimrod his second was he.For his breakfast he'd take a large venison steak,And despis'd your slip-slops and tea, my brave boys.

9.

While all in a row, with squaw, dog and bow,Vermilion adorning his face,With feathery head he rang'd the woods wide:*St. George* sure had never such grace, my brave boys?

10.

His jetty black hair, such as Buckskin saints wear,Perfumed with bear's grease well smear'd,Which illum'd the saint's face, and ran down apace,Like the oil from Aaron's old beard, my brave boys.

11.

The strong nervous deer, with amazing career,In swiftness he'd fairly run down;And, like Sampson, wou'd tear wolf, lion or bear.Ne'er was such a saint as our own, my brave boys.[Pg 323]

12.

When he'd run down a stag, he behind him wou'd lag;For, so noble a soul had he!He'd stop, tho' he lost it, tradition reports it,To give him fresh chance to get free, my brave boys.

13.

With a mighty strong arm, and a masculine bow,His arrow he drew to the head,And as sure as he shot, it was ever his lot,His prey it fell instantly dead, my brave boys.

14.

His table he spread where the venison bled,Be thankful, he used to say;He'd laugh and he'd sing, tho' a saint and a king,And sumptuously dine on his prey, my brave boys.

15.

Then over the hills, o'er the mountains and rillsHe'd caper, such was his delight;And ne'er in his days, Indian history says,Did lack a good supper at night, my brave boys.

16.

On an old stump he sat, without cap or hat.When supper was ready to eat,*Snap*, his dog, he stood by, and cast a sheep's eyeFor ven'son, the king of all meat, my brave boys.

17.

Like Isaac of old, and both cast in one mould,Tho' a wigwam was Tamm'ny's cottage,He lov'd sav'ry meat, such that patriarchs eat,Of ven'son and squirrel made pottage, brave boys.

18.

When fourscore years old, as I've oft'times been told,To doubt it, sure, would not be right,With a pipe in his jaw, he'd buss his old squaw,And get a young saint ev'ry night, my brave boys.[Pg 324]

19.

As old age came on, he grew blind, deaf and dumb,Tho' his sport, 'twere hard to keep from it,Quite tired of life, bid adieu to his wife,And blazed like the tail of a comet, brave boys.

20.

What country on earth, then, did ever give birthTo such a magnanimous saint?His acts far excel all that history tell,And language too feeble to paint, my brave boys.

21.

Now, to finish my song, a full flowing bowlI'll quaff, and sing all the long day,And with punch and wine paint my cheeks for my saint,And hail ev'ry First of sweet *May*, my brave boys.

DICK. What a seraphic voice! how it enlivens my soul! Come away, away, Roger, the moments are precious.

[*Exeunt* DICK *and* ROGER.

SCENE VII. *In a chamber, near Boston, the morning after the battle of Bunkers-Hill.*

CLARISSA. How lovely is this new-born day!—The sun rises with uncommon radiance after the most gloomy night my wearied eyes ever knew.—The voice of slumber was not heard—the angel of sleep was fled—and the awful whispers of solemnity and silence prevented my eye-lids from closing.—No wonder—the terrors and ideas of yesterday—such a scene of war—of tumult—hurry and hubbub—of horror and destruction—the direful noise of conflict—the dismal hissing of iron shot in volleys flying—such bellowing of mortars—such thund'ring of cannon—such roaring of musketry—and such clashing of swords and bayonets—such cries of the wounded—and such streams of blood—such a noise and crush of houses, steeples, and whole streets of desolate Charlestown falling—pillars of fire, and the convulsed vortex of fiery flakes, rolling in flaming wreaths in the air, in dreadful combustion, seemed as tho' the elements and whole earth were envelop'd in one general, eternal conflagration and total ruin, and intermingled with black smoke, ascending, on the wings of mourning, up to Heaven, seemed piteously to implore the Al[Pg 325]mighty interposition to put a stop to such devastation, lest the whole earth should be unpeopled in the unnatural conflict—Too, too much for female heroism to dwell upon—But what are all those to the terrors that filled my affrighted imagination the last night?—Dreams—fancies—evil bodings—shadows, phantoms and ghastly visions continually hovering around my pillow, goading and harrowing my soul with the most terrific appearances, not imaginary, but real—Am I awake?—Where are the British murderers?—where's my husband?—my son?—my brother?—Something more than human tells me all is not well: If they are among the slain, 'tis impossible.—I—Oh! [*She cries.*]

Enter a NEIGHBOUR [*a spectator of the battle*].

NEIGHBOUR. Madam, grieve not so much.

CLARISSA. Am I wont to grieve without a cause? Wou'd to God I did;—mock me not—What voice is that? methinks I know it—some angel sent to comfort me?—welcome then. [*She turns about.*] Oh, my Neighbour, is it you? My friend, I have need of comfort. Hast thou any for me?—say—will you not speak? Where's my husband?—my son?—my brother? Hast thou seen them since the battle? Oh! bring me not unwelcome tidings! [*Cries.*]

NEIGHBOUR. [*Aside. What shall I say?*] Madam, I beheld them yesterday from an eminence.

CLARISSA. Upon that very eminence was I. What then?—

NEIGHBOUR. I saw the brave man Warren, your son and brother.

CLARISSA. What? O ye gods!—Speak on friend—stop—what saw ye?

NEIGHBOUR. In the midst of the tempest of war—

CLARISSA. Where are they now?—That I saw too—What is all this?

NEIGHBOUR. Madam, hear me—

CLARISSA. Then say on—yet—Oh, his looks!—I fear!

NEIGHBOUR. When General Putnam bid the vanguard open their front to the—

CLARISSA. Oh, trifle not with me—dear Neighbour!—where shall I find them?—say—

NEIGHBOUR. [*Aside. Heavens! must I tell her!*] Madam, be patient—right and left, that all may see who hate us, we are prepar'd for them[Pg 326]—

CLARISSA. What then?—Can you find 'em?—

NEIGHBOUR. I saw Warren and the other two heroes firm as Roxbury stand the shock of the enemy's fiercest attacks, and twice put to flight their boasted phalanx.—

CLARISSA. All that I saw, and more; say—wou'd they not come to me, were they well?—

NEIGHBOUR. Madam, hear me—

CLARISSA. Oh! he will not speak.

NEIGHBOUR. The enemy return'd to the charge, and stumbling o'er the dead and wounded bodies of their friends, Warren received them with indissoluble firmness, and notwithstanding their battalious aspect, in the midst of the battle, tho' surrounded with foes on ev'ry side—

CLARISSA. Oh, my Neighbour!—

NEIGHBOUR. Madam—his nervous arm, like a giant refresh'd with wine, hurl'd destruction where'er he came, breathing heroic ardour to advent'rous deeds, and long time in even scale the battle hung, till at last death turn'd pale and affrighted at the carnage—they ran—

CLARISSA. Who ran?

NEIGHBOUR. The enemy, Madam, gave way—

CLARISSA. Warren never ran—yet—oh! I wou'd he had—I fear—[*Cries.*]

NEIGHBOUR. I say not so, Madam.

CLARISSA. What say ye then? he was no coward, Neighbour—

NEIGHBOUR. Brave to the last. [*Aside. I forgot myself.*]

CLARISSA. What said you? O Heavens! brave to the last! those words—why do you keep me thus?—cruel—

NEIGHBOUR. [*Aside. She will know it.*] I say, Madam, by some mistaken orders on our side, the enemy rallied and return'd to the charge with fresh numbers, and your husband, son, and brother—Madam—

CLARISSA. Stop!—O ye powers!—What?—say no more—yet let me hear—keep me not thus—tell me, I charge thee—

NEIGHBOUR. [*Aside. I can hold no longer, she must know it.*] Forgive me, Madam—I saw them fall—and Michael, the archangel, who vanquish'd Satan, is not more immortal than they. [*Aside. Who can relate such woes without a tear?*],

CLARISSA. Oh! I've heard enough—too—too much [*Cries.*] yet—if thou hast worse to tell—say on—nought worse can be—O ye gods!—cruel—cruel—thrice cruel—cou'd ye not leave[Pg 327] me one—[*She faints, and is caught by her friend, and placed in a chair; he rings the bell, the family come in, and endeavour to bring her to.*]

NEIGHBOUR. With surprising fortitude she heard the melancholy relation, until I came to the last close—she then gave me a mournful look, lifted up her eyes, and immediately sunk motionless into my arms.

14

WOMAN. Poor soul!—no wonder—how I sympathize with her in her distress—my tender bosom can scarcely bear the sight! A dreadful loss! a most shocking scene it was, that brothers should with brothers war, and in intestine fierce opposition meet, to seek the blood of each other, like dogs for a bare bone, who so oft in generous friendship and commerce join'd, in festivals of love and joy unanimous as the sons of one kind and indulgent father, and separately would freely in a good cause spend their blood and sacrifice their lives for him.

NEIGHBOUR. A terrible black day it was, and ever will be remembered by New-England, when that vile Briton (unworthy the name of a Briton), Lord Boston (curse the name!), whose horrid murders stain American soil with blood; perish his name! a fratricide! 'twas he who fir'd Charlestown, and spread desolation, fire, flames and smoke in ev'ry corner—he was the wretch, that waster of the world, that licens'd robber, that blood-stain'd insulter of a free people, who bears the name of Lord Boston, but from henceforth shall be called Cain, that pillag'd the ruins, and dragg'd and murder'd the infant, the aged and infirm—(But look, she recovers.)

CLARISSA. O ye angels! ye cherubims and seraphims! waft their souls to bliss, bathe their wounds with angelic balsam, and crown them with immortality. A faithful, loving and beloved husband, a promising and filial son, a tender and affectionate brother. Alas! what a loss!—Whom have I now to comfort me?—What have I left, but the voice of lamentation: [*She weeps.*] Ill-fated bullets—these tears shall sustain me—yes, ye dear friends! how gladly wou'd I follow you—but alas! I must still endure tribulation and inquietudes, from which you are now exempt; I cannot cease to weep, ye brave men, I will mourn your fall—weep on—flow, mine eyes, and wash away their blood, till the fountain of sorrow is dried up—but, oh! it never—never will—my sympathetic soul shall dwell on your bosoms, and floods of tears shall water your graves; and since all other[Pg 328]comfort is deny'd me, deprive me not of the only consolation left me of meditating on your virtues and dear memories, who fell in defense of liberty and your country—ye brave men—ye more than friends—ye martyrs to liberty!—This, this is all I ask, till sorrow overwhelms me.—I breathe my last; and ye yourselves, your own bright spirits, come and waft me to your peaceful abode, where the voice of lamentation is not heard, neither shall we know any more what it is to separate.

Eager the patriot meets his desperate foeWith full intent to give the fatal blow;The cause he fights for animates him high,His wife, his children and his liberty.For these he conquers, or more bravely dies,And yields himself a willing sacrifice.

[*Exeunt.*

ACT IV.

SCENE I. *Near Norfolk, in Virginia, on board a man-of-war,* LORD KIDNAPPER, *in the state-room; a boat appears rowing towards the ship.*
SAILOR *and* BOATSWAIN.

SAILOR. Boatswain!
BOATSWAIN. Holla.
SAILOR. Damn my eyes, Mr. Boatswain, but here's a black flag of truce coming on board.
BOATSWAIN. Sure enough—where are they from?
SAILOR. From hell, I suppose—for they're as black as so many devils.
BOATSWAIN. Very well—no matter—they're recruits for the Kidnapper.
SAILOR. We shall be all of a colour by and by—damn me—
BOATSWAIN. I'll go and inform his Lordship and his pair of doxies of it; I suppose by this time they have trim'd their sails, and he's done heaving the log.

[*Exit* BOATSWAIN.

SCENE II. *Near the state-room.*

BOATSWAIN. Where's his Lordship?
SERVANT. He's in the state-room.
BOATSWAIN. It's time for him to turn out; tell him I want to speak to him.
SERVANT. I dare not do it, Boatswain; it's more than my life is worth.[Pg 329]
BOATSWAIN. Damn your squeamish stomach, go directly, or I'll go myself.
SERVANT. For God's sake! Boatswain—
BOATSWAIN. Damn your eyes, you pimping son of a bitch, go this instant, or I'll stick my knife in your gammons.
SERVANT. O Lord! Boatswain. [SERVANT *goes.*]
BOATSWAIN [*solus*]. What the devil—keep a pimp guard here, better station the son of a bitch at the mast head, to keep a look out there, lest Admiral Hopkins be upon us.

Enter KIDNAPPER.

KIDNAPPER. What's your will, Boatswain?
BOATSWAIN. I beg your Lordship's pardon [*Aside. But you can soon fetch up Leeway, and spread the water sail again.*], please your honour, here's a boat full of fine recruits along side for you.
KIDNAPPER. Recruits, Boatswain? you mean soldiers from Augustine, I imagine; what reg'mentals have they on?
BOATSWAIN. Mourning, please your honour, and as black as our tarpawling.
KIDNAPPER. Ha, ha, well well, take 'em on board, Boatswain, I'll be on deck presently.
BOATSWAIN. With submission to your honour, d' ye see, [*Scratching his head.*] I think we have gallows-looking dogs enough on board already—the scrapings of Newgate, and the refuse of Tyburn, and when the wind blows aft, damn 'em, they stink like polecats—but d' ye see, as your honour pleases, with submission, if it's Lord Paramount's orders, why it must be so, I suppose—but I've done my duty, d' ye see—
KIDNAPPER. Ha, ha, the work must be done, Boatswain, no matter by whom.
BOATSWAIN. Why, aye, that's true, please your honour, any port in a storm—if a man is to be hang'd, or have his throat cut, d' ye see—who are so fit to do it as his own slaves? especially as they're to have their freedoms for it; nobody can blame 'em, nor your honour neither, for you get them for half price, or nothing at all, d' ye see me, and that will help to lessen poor Owld England's taxes, and when you have done with 'em here, and they get their brains knock'd out, d' ye see, your honour can sell them in the West-Indies, and that will be something in your honour's pocket, d' ye see—well, ev'ry man to his trade—but, damn my impudence for all, I see your honour knows all about it—d' ye see.

[*Exit* BOATSWAIN.

[Pg 330]

SCENE III. LORD KIDNAPPER *returns to his state-room; the* BOATSWAIN *comes on deck and pipes.*
All hands ahoy—hand a rope, some of you Tories, forward there, for his worship's reg'ment of black guards to come aboard.

Enter NEGROES.

BOATSWAIN. Your humble servant, Gentlemen, I suppose you want to see Lord Kidnapper?—Clear the gangway there of them Tyburn tulips. Please to walk aft, brother soldiers, that's the fittest birth for you, the Kidnapper's in the state-room, he'll hoist his sheet-anchor presently, he'll be up in a jiffin—as soon as he has made fast the end of his small rope athwart Jenny Bluegarter and Kate Common's stern posts.

15

FIRST SAILOR. Damn my eyes, but I suppose, messmate, we must bundle out of our hammocks this cold weather, to make room for these black regulars to stow in, tumble upon deck, and choose a soft berth among the snow?

SECOND SAILOR. Blast 'em, if they come within a cable's length of my hammock, I'll kick 'em to hell through one of the gun ports.

BOATSWAIN. Come, come, brothers, don't be angry, I suppose we shall soon be in a warmer latitude—the Kidnapper seems as fond of these black regulars (as you call 'em, Jack) as he is of the brace of whores below; but as they come in so damn'd slow, I'll put him in the humour of sending part of the fleet this winter to the coast of Guinea, and beat up for volunteers, there he'll get recruits enough for a hogshead or two of New-England rum, and a few owld pipe-shanks, and save poor Owld-England the trouble and expense of clothing them in the bargain.

FIRST SAILOR. Aye, BOATSWAIN, any voyage, so it's a warm one—if it's to hell itself—for I'm sure the devil must be better off than we, if we are to stay here this winter.

SECOND SAILOR. Any voyage, so it's to the southward, rather than stay here at lazy anchor—no fire, nothing to eat or drink, but suck our frosty fists like bears, unless we turn sheep-stealers again, and get our brains knock'd out. Eigh, master cook, you're a gentleman now—nothing to do—grown so proud, you won't speak to poor folks, I suppose?

COOK. The devil may cook for 'em for me—if I had any thing to cook—a parcel of frozen half-starv'd dogs. I should never be able to keep 'em out of the cook room, or their noses out of the slush-tub.[Pg 331]

BOATSWAIN. Damn your old smoky jaws, you're better off than any man aboard, your trouble will be nothing,—for I suppose they'll be disbursted in different messes among the Tories, and it's only putting on the big pot, cockey. Ha, ha, ha.

COOK. What signifies, Mr. Boatswain, the big pot or the little pot, if there's nothing to cook? no fire, coal or wood to cook with? Blast my eyes, Mr. Boatswain, if I disgrease myself so much, I have had the honour, damn me (tho' I say it that shou'dn't say it) to be chief cook of a seventy-four gun ship, on board of which was Lord Abel-Marl and Admiral Poke-Cock.

BOATSWAIN. Damn the liars—old singe-the-devil—you chief cook of a seventy-four gun ship, eigh? you the devil, you're as proud as hell, for all you look as old as Matheg'lum, hand a pair of silk stockings for our cook here, d' ye see—lash a handspike athwart his arse, get a ladle full of slush and a handful of brimstone for his hair, and step one of you Tories there for the devil's barber to come and shave and dress him. Ha, ha, ha.

COOK. No, Mr. Boatswain, it's not pride—but look 'e (as I said before), I'll not disgrease my station, I'll throw up my commission, before I'll stand cook for a parcel of scape gallows, convict Tory dogs and run-away Negroes.

BOATSWAIN. What's that you say? Take care, old frosty face—What? do you accuse his worship of turning kidnapper, and harbouring run-away Negroes?—Softly, or you'll be taken up for a Whig, and get a handsome coat of slush and hog's feathers for a christmas-box, cockey: Throw up your commission, eigh? throw up the pot-halliards, you mean, old piss-to-windward? Ha, ha, ha.

COOK. I tell you, Mr. Boatswain—I—

BOATSWAIN. Come, come, give us a chaw of tobacco, Cook— blast your eyes, don't take any pride in what I say—I'm only joking, d' ye see——

COOK. Well, but Mr. Boatswain——

BOATSWAIN. Come, avast, belay the lanyards of your jaws, and let's have no more of it, d' ye see. [BOATSWAIN *pipes*.] Make fast that boat along side there.

[*Exeunt ev'ry man to his station.*]

SCENE IV. LORD KIDNAPPER *comes up on the quarter-deck.*

KIDNAPPER. Well, my brave blacks, are you come to list?

CUDJO. Eas, massa Lord, you preazee.

KIDNAPPER. How many are there of you?[Pg 332]

CUDJO. Twenty-two, massa.

KIDNAPPER. Very well, did you all run away from your masters?

CUDJO. Eas, massa Lord, eb'ry one, me too.

KIDNAPPER. That's clever; they have no right to make you slaves, I wish all the Negroes wou'd do the same, I'll make 'em free—what part did you come from?

CUDJO. Disse brack man, disse one, disse one, disse one, disse one, come from Hamton, disse one, disse one, disse one, come from Nawfok, me come from Nawfok too.

KIDNAPPER. Very well, what was your master's name?

CUDJO. Me massa name Cunney Tomsee.

KIDNAPPER. Colonel Thompson—eigh?

CUDJO. Eas, massa, Cunney Tomsee.

KIDNAPPER. Well then I'll make you a major—and what's your name?

CUDJO. Me massa cawra me Cudjo.

KIDNAPPER. Cudjo?—very good—was you ever christened, Cudjo?

CUDJO. No massa, me no crissen.

KIDNAPPER. Well, then I'll christen you—you shall be called Major Cudjo Thompson, and if you behave well, I'll soon make you a greater man than your master, and if I find the rest of you behave well, I'll make you all officers, and after you have serv'd Lord Paramount a while, you shall have money in your pockets, good clothes on your backs, and be as free as them white men there. [*Pointing forward to a parcel of Tories.*]

CUDJO. Tankee, massa, gaw bresse, massa Kidnap.

SAILOR. [*Aside.*] What a damn'd big mouth that Cudjo has—as large as our main hatch-way——

COOK. [*Aside.*] Aye, he's come to a wrong place to make a good use of it—it might stand some little chance at a Lord Mayor's feast.

KIDNAPPER. Now go forward, give 'em something to eat and drink there. [*Aside.*] Poor devils, they look half starved and naked like ourselves.

COOK. [*Aside.*] I don't know where the devil they'll get it: the sight of that fellow's mouth is enough to breed a famine on board, if there was not one already.

SAILOR. Aye, he'd tumble plenty down his damn'd guts and swallow it, like Jones swallow'd the whale.[Pg 333]

KIDNAPPER. To-morrow you shall have guns like them white men—Can you shoot some of them rebels ashore, Major Cudjo?

CUDJO. Eas, massa, me try.

KIDNAPPER. Wou'd you shoot your old master, the Colonel, if you could see him?

CUDJO. Eas, massa, you terra me, me shoot him down dead.

KIDNAPPER. That's a brave fellow—damn 'em—down with them all—shoot all the damn'd rebels.

SERJEANT. [*Aside.*] Brave fellows indeed!

KIDNAPPER. Serjeant!

SERJEANT. I wait your Lordship's commands.

KIDNAPPER. Serjeant, to-morrow begin to teach those black recruits the exercise, and when they have learn'd sufficiently well to load and fire, then incorporate them among the regulars and the other Whites on board; we shall in a few days have some work for 'em, I expect—be as expeditious as possible. [*Aside to him.*] Set a guard over them every night, and take their arms from them, for who knows but they may cut our throats.

SERJEANT. Very true, My Lord, I shall take particular care.

[Exit KIDNAPPER*;* SERJEANT *and* NEGROES *walk forward.*

SCENE V.

SERJEANT. Damn 'em, I'd rather see half their weight in beef.

BOATSWAIN. Aye, curse their stomachs, or mutton either; then our Cook wou'dn't be so damn'd lazy as he is, strutting about the deck like a nobleman, receiving Paramount's pay for nothing.

SERJEANT. Walk faster, damn your black heads. I suppose, Boatswain, when this hell-cat reg'ment's complete, they'll be reviewed in Hyde park?——

BOATSWAIN. Aye, blast my eyes, and our Chaplain with his dirty black gown, or our Cook, shall be their general, and review 'em, for he talks of throwing up his pot-halliards commission, in hopes of it.

SERJEANT. Ha, ha, ha.——

COOK. I'd see the devil have 'em first.——

[Exeunt SERJEANT, *&c.*

SCENE VI. *In the cabin.*

LORD KIDNAPPER, CAPTAIN SQUIRES, *and* CHAPLAIN.

KIDNAPPER. These blacks are no small acquisition, them and the Tories we have on board will strengthen us vastly; the[Pg 334] thoughts of emancipation will make 'em brave, and the encouragement given them by my proclamation, will greatly intimidate the rebels—internal enemies are worse than open foes.——

CHAPLAIN. Very true, My Lord; David prayed that he might be preserved from secret enemies.

KIDNAPPER. Aye, so I've heard, but I look upon this to be a grand manœuvre in politics; this is making dog eat dog—thief catch thief—the servant against his master—rebel against rebel—what think you of that, parson?

CHAPLAIN. A house divided thus against itself cannot stand, according to scripture—My Lord, your observation is truly scriptural.

KIDNAPPER. Scripture? poh, poh—I've nothing to do with scripture—I mean politically, parson.

CHAPLAIN. I know it very well; sure, My Lord, I understand you perfectly.

KIDNAPPER. Faith that's all I care for; if we can stand our ground this winter, and burn all their towns that are accessible to our ships, and Colonel Connolly succeeds in his plan, there's not the least doubt but we shall have supplies from England very early in the spring, which I have wrote for; then, in conjunction with Connolly, we shall be able to make a descent where we please, and drive the rebels like hogs into a pen.

CHAPLAIN. And then gather them (as the scriptures say) as a hen gathereth her chickens.

KIDNAPPER. True, Mr. Scripture.

CAPTAIN SQUIRES. Very good, but you must take care of the hawks.

KIDNAPPER. What do you mean by the hawks, Captain?

CAPTAIN SQUIRES. I mean the shirt-men, the rifle-men, My Lord.

KIDNAPPER. Aye, damn 'em, hawks indeed; they are cursed dogs; a man is never safe where they are, but I'll take care to be out of their reach, let others take their chance, for I see they have no respect to persons—I suppose they wou'd shoot at me, if I were within their reach.

CHAPLAIN. Undoubtedly, they would be more fond of you than of a wild turkey; a parcel of ignorant, unmannerly rascals, they pay no more respect to a Lord than they wou'd to a devil.

KIDNAPPER. The scoundrels are grown so damn'd impudent too, that one can scarcely get a roasting pig now-a-days, but I'll be even with some of 'em by and by.[Pg 335]

CHAPLAIN. I hope we shall get something good for our Christmas dinner—so much abstinence and involuntary mortification, cannot be good for the soul—a war in the body corporal is of more dangerous consequence than a civil war to the state, or heresy and schism to the church.

KIDNAPPER. Very true, parson—very true—now I like your doctrine—a full belly is better than an empty sermon; preach that doctrine;—stick to that text, and you'll not fail of making converts.

CHAPLAIN. The wisest of men said, there is nothing better, than that a man should enjoy that which he hath, namely, eat, drink, and be merry, if he can.

KIDNAPPER. You're very right—Solomon was no fool, they say—[*He sings.*]
Give me a charming lass, Twangdillo cries,
I know no pleasure, but love's sweet joys.

CHAPLAIN. [*Sings.*]
Give me the bottle, says the red face sot,
For a whore I'd not give six-pence, not a groat.

Yet two is better than one, my Lord, for the scriptures further say, if one be alone, how can there be heat? You seem to be converted to that belief, for you have a brace of them, as the Boatswain says.

KIDNAPPER. Ha, ha. It's a pity but you were a bishop, you have the scriptures so pat—now I'll go and take a short nap, meanwhile; Captain, if any thing new happens, pray order my servant to wake me.

CAPTAIN SQUIRES. I will, my Lord.

[Exit KIDNAPPER.

CHAPLAIN. And you and I'll crack a bottle, Captain; (bring a bottle, boy!) 'tis bad enough to perish by famine, but ten thousand times worse to be chok'd for want of moisture. His Lordship and two more make three; and you and I and the bottle make three more, and a three-fold cord is not easily broken; so we're even with him.

CAPTAIN SQUIRES. With all my heart.—Boy, bear a hand!

TOM. Coming, sir.

CHAPLAIN. Tom, Tom!—make haste, you scoundrel!—fetch two bottles. I think we can manage it.[Pg 336]

Enter TOM *with the bottles.*

CHAPLAIN. That's right, Tom.—Now bring the glasses, and shut the door after you.

[Exit TOM.

SCENE VII. *In Boston. A council of war after the battle of Bunker's-Hill.*

LORD BOSTON, ADMIRAL TOMBSTONE, ELBOW ROOM, MR. CAPER, GENERAL CLINTON, EARL PERCY.

LORD BOSTON. I fully expected, with the help of the last reinforcement you brought me over, and the advice and assistance of three accomplish'd and experienc'd Generals, I should have been able to have subdued the rebels, and gain'd immortal laurels to myself—have return'd to Old England like a Roman Consul, with a score or two of the rebel Generals, Colonels and Majors, to have grac'd my triumph.

ELBOW ROOM. You have been vastly disappointed, sir—you must not look for laurels (unless wild ones) nor expect triumphs (unless sham ones) from your own victories or conquests in America.

LORD BOSTON. And yet, not more disappointed than you, sir—witness your thrasonical speeches on your first landing, provided you had but elbow room—and Mr. Caper too, to bring over Monsieur Rigadoon, the dancing-master, and Signor Rosin, the fiddler forsooth; he thought, no doubt, to have country danc'd the rebels out of their liberty with some of his new cuts—with his soft music to have fascinated their wives and daughters, and with some of 'em, no doubt, to have taken the tour of America, with his reg'ment of fine, sleek, prancing horses, that have been feeding this six months on our crackers tails; he thought to have grown fat with feasting, dancing, and drinking tea with the Ladies, instead of being the skeleton he now appears to be—not to mention any thing of his letter, wherein he laments Tom's absence; for[2] "had Tom been with him (he says) he wou'd have been out of danger, and quite secure from the enemy's shot."

PERCY. I think, Gentlemen, we're even with you now; you have had your mirth and frolic with us, for dancing "Yankee Doodle," as you called it, from Lexington.—I find you have had a severer dance, a brave sweat at Bunker's Hill, and have been obliged to pay the fiddler in the bargain.

[Pg 337]

CLINTON. However, Gentlemen, I approve (at proper seasons) of a little joking, yet I can by no means think (as we have had such bad success with our crackers) that this is a proper time to throw your squibs.

LORD BOSTON. I grant you, sir, this is a very improper time for joking; for my part, I was only speaking as to my own thoughts, when Mr. Elbow Room made remarks, which he might as well have spared.

ELBOW ROOM. I took you, sir, as meaning a reflection upon us for our late great loss, and particularly to myself, for expressing some surprise on our first landing, that you should suffer a parcel of ignorant peasants to drive you before 'em like sheep from Lexington; and I must own I was a little chagrin'd at your seeming so unconcern'd at such an affair as this (which had nearly prov'd our ruin), by your innuendoes and ironical talk of accomplish'd Generals, Roman Consuls and triumphs.

LORD BOSTON. My mentioning accomplish'd Generals, surely, sir, was rather a compliment to you.

ELBOW ROOM. When irony pass current for compliments, and we take it so, I shall have no objection to it.

MR. CAPER. The affair of Lexington, My Lord Boston, at which you were so much affrighted (if I am rightly inform'd), was because you then stood on your own bottom, this of Bunker's Hill you seem secretly to rejoice at, only because you have three accomplish'd and experienc'd Generals to share the disgrace with you, besides the brave Admiral Tombstone—you talk of dancing and fiddling, and yet you do neither, as I see.

LORD BOSTON. And pray, sir, what did you do with the commission, the post, the Duke of Grafton gave you, in lieu of your losses at Preston election, and the expenses of your trial at the king's bench for a riot, which had emptied your pockets?—Why you sold it—you sold it, sir—to raise cash to gamble with.——

ADMIRAL TOMBSTONE. Damn it, don't let us kick up a dust among ourselves, to be laugh'd at fore and aft—this is a hell of a council of war—though I believe it will turn out one before we've done—a scolding and quarrelling like a parcel of damn'd butter whores—I never heard two whores yet scold and quarrel, but they got to fighting at last.

CLINTON. Pray, Gentlemen, drop this discourse, consider the honour of England is at stake, and our own safety depends upon this day's consultation.[Pg 338]

LORD BOSTON. 'Tis not for argument's sake—but the dignity of my station requires others should give up first.

ELBOW ROOM. Sir, I have done, lest you should also accuse me of obstructing the proceedings of the council of war.

MR. CAPER. For the same reason I drop it now.

LORD BOSTON. Well, Gentlemen, what are we met here for?

ADMIRAL TOMBSTONE. Who the devil shou'd know, if you don't?—damn it, didn't you send for us?

LORD BOSTON. Our late great loss of men has tore up the foundation of our plan, and render'd all further attempts impracticable—'t will be a long time ere we can expect any more reinforcements—and if they should arrive, I'm doubtful of their success.

CLINTON. The provincials are vastly strong, and seem no novices in the art of war; 'tis true we gain'd the hill at last, but of what advantage is it to us?—none—the loss of 1400 as brave men as Britain can boast of, is a melancholy consideration, and must make our most sanguinary friends in England abate of their vigour.

ELBOW ROOM. I never saw or read of any battle equal to it—never was more martial courage display'd, and the provincials, to do the dogs justice, fought like heroes, fought indeed more like devils than men; such carnage and destruction not exceeded by Blenheim, Minden, Fontenoy, Ramillies, Dettingen, the battle of the Boyne, and the late affair of the Spaniards and Algerines—a mere cock-fight to it—no laurels there.

MR. CAPER. No, nor triumphs neither—I regret in particular the number of brave officers that fell that day, many of whom were of the first families in England.

ADMIRAL TOMBSTONE. Aye, a damn'd affair indeed—many powder'd beaus—petit maitres—fops—fribbles—skip jacks—macaronies—jack puddings—noblemen's bastards and whores' sons fell that day—and my poor marines stood no more chance with 'em than a cat in hell without claws.

LORD BOSTON. It can't be help'd, Admiral; what is to be done next?

ADMIRAL TOMBSTONE. Done?—why, what the devil have you done? nothing yet, but eat Paramount's beef, and steal a few Yankee sheep—and that, it seems, is now become a damn'd lousy, beggarly trade too, for you hav'n't left yourselves a mouthful to eat.[Pg 339]

[*Aside.*]

"*Bold at the council board,But cautious in the field, he shunn'd the sword.*"

LORD BOSTON. But what can we do, Admiral?

ADMIRAL TOMBSTONE. Do?—why, suck your paws—that's all you're like to get. [*Aside.*] But avast, I must bowse taught there, or we shall get to loggerheads soon, we're such damn'd fighting fellows.

LORD BOSTON. We must act on the defensive this winter, till reinforcements arrive.

ADMIRAL TOMBSTONE. Defensive? aye, aye—if we can defend our bellies from hunger, and prevent a mutiny and civil war among the small guts there this winter, we shall make a glorious campaign of it, indeed—it will read well in the American Chronicles.

LORD BOSTON. I expect to be recalled this winter, when I shall lay the case before Lord Paramount, and let him know your deplorable situation.

ADMIRAL TOMBSTONE. Aye, do—and lay it behind him too; you've got the weather-gage of us this tack, messmate; but I wish you a good voyage for all—and don't forget to tell him, the poor worms are starving too, having nothing to eat, but half starv'd dead soldiers and the ships' bottoms. [*Aside.*] A cunning old fox, he's gnaw'd his way handsomely out of the Boston cage—but he'll never be a *wolf*, for all that.

MR. CAPER. I shall desire to be recalled too—I've not been us'd to such fare—and not the least diversion or entertainment of any sort going forward here—I neither can nor will put up with it.

ADMIRAL TOMBSTONE. I think we're all a parcel of damn'd boobies for coming three thousand miles upon a wild-goose chase—to perish with cold—starve with hunger—get our brains knock'd out, or be hang'd for sheep-stealing and robbing hen-roosts.

18

LORD BOSTON. I think, Admiral, you're always grumbling—never satisfied.

ADMIRAL TOMBSTONE. Satisfied? I see no appearance of it—we have been here these twelve hours, scolding upon empty stomachs—you may call it a council of war (and so it is indeed, a war with the guts) or what you will—but I call it a council of famine.[Pg 340]

LORD BOSTON. As it's so late, Gentlemen, we'll adjourn the council of war till to-morrow at nine o'clock—I hope you'll all attend, and come to a conclusion.

ADMIRAL TOMBSTONE. And I hope you'll then conclude to favour us with one of them fine turkeys you're keeping for your sea store [*Aside.*] or that fine, fat, black pig you or some of your guard stole out of the poor Negroe's pen. As it's near Christmas, and you're going to make your exit—you know the old custom among the sailors—pave your way first—let us have one good dinner before we part, and leave us half a dozen pipes of Mr. Hancock's wine to drink your health, and a good voyage, and don't let us part with dry lips.

Such foolish councils, with no wisdom fraught,Must end in wordy words, and come to nought;Just like St. James's, where they bluster, scold,They nothing know—yet they despise being told.

[*Exeunt.*

FOOTNOTES:

[9]See Burgoyne's letter.

ACT V.
SCENE I. *At Montreal.*
GENERAL PRESCOT *and* OFFICER.
GENERAL PRESCOT.

So it seems indeed, one misfortune seldom comes alone.—The rebels, after the taking of Ticonderoga and Chamblee, as I just now learn by a Savage, marched immediately to besiege St. John's, and are now before that place, closely investing it, and no doubt intend paying us a visit soon.

OFFICER. Say you so? then 'tis time to look about us.

GEN. PRESCOT. They'll find us prepar'd, I'll warrant 'em, to give 'em such a reception as they little dream of—a parcel of Yankee dogs.

OFFICER. Their success, no doubt, has elated them, and given 'em hopes of conquering all Canada soon, if that's their intent.

GEN. PRESCOT. No doubt it is—but I'll check their career a little.—[Pg 341]—

Enter SCOUTING OFFICER, *with* COLONEL ALLEN, *and other prisoners.*

SCOUTING OFFICER. Sir, I make bold to present you with a few prisoners—they are a scouting detachment from the army besieging St. John's.

GEN. PRESCOT. Prisoners? Rebels, I suppose, and scarcely worth hanging.

COL. ALLEN. Sir, you suppose wrong—you mean scarcely worth your while to attempt.

GEN. PRESCOT. Pray, who are you, sir?

COL. ALLEN. A man, sir, and who had the honour, till now, to command those brave men, whom you call rebels.

GEN. PRESCOT. What is your name? If I may be so bold?

COL. ALLEN. Allen.

GEN. PRESCOT. Allen?

COL. ALLEN. Yes, Allen.

GEN. PRESCOT. Are you that Allen, that Colonel Allen (as they call him) that dar'd to take Ticonderoga?

COL. ALLEN. The same—the very man.

GEN. PRESCOT. Then rebels you are, and as such I shall treat you, for daring to oppose Lord Paramount's troops, and the laws of the land.

COL. ALLEN. Prisoners we are, 'tis true—but we despise the name of a rebel—With more propriety that name is applicable to your master—'tis he who attempts to destroy the laws of the land, not us—we mean to support them, and defend our property against Paramount's and parliamentary tyranny.

GEN. PRESCOT. To answer you were a poorness of spirit I despise; when rebels dare accuse, power that replies, forgets to punish; I am not to argue that point with you: And let me tell you, sir, whoever you are, it now ill becomes you thus to talk—You're my prisoner—your life is in my hands, and you shall suffer immediately—Guards! take them away.

COL. ALLEN. Cruel insult!—pardon these brave men!—what they have done has been by my orders—I am the only guilty person (if guilt there be), let me alone suffer for them all. [*Opening his breast.*] Here! take your revenge—Why do you hesitate?—Will you not strike a breast that ne'er will flinch from your pointed bayonet?

GEN. PRESCOT. Provoke me not—Remember you're my prisoners.[Pg 342]

COL. ALLEN. Our souls are free!—Strike, cowards, strike!—I scorn to beg my life.

GEN. PRESCOT. Guards! away with them—I'll reserve you for a more ignominious death—your fate is fix'd—away with them.

COL. ALLEN. [*Going off.*] Be glutted, ye thirsters after human blood—Come, see me suffer—mark my eye, and scorn me, if my expiring soul confesses fear—Come, see and be taught virtue, and to die as a patriot for the wrongs of my country.

[*Exeunt* PRISONERS *and* GUARDS.

SCENE II. *A Dungeon.*

COL. ALLEN. What! ye infernal monsters! murder us in the dark?—What place is this?—Who reigns king of these gloomy mansions?—You might favour us at least with one spark of light—Ye cannot see to do your business here.

OFFICER. 'Tis our orders.

COL. ALLEN. Ye dear, ye brave, wretched friends!—now would I die for ye all—ye share a death I wou'd gladly excuse you from—'Tis not death I fear—this is only bodily death—but to die noteless in the silent dark, is to die scorn'd, and shame our suff'ring country—we fall undignify'd by villains' hands—a sacrifice to Britain's outcast blood-hounds—This, this shakes the soul!—Come then, ye murderers, since it must be so—do your business speedily—Farewell, my friends! to die with you is now my noblest claim since to die for you was a choice deny'd—What are ye about?—Stand off, ye wretches!

OFFICER. I am order'd to lay you in irons. [*They seize him.*] You must submit.

COL. ALLEN. What, do you mean to torture us to death with chains, racks and gibbets? rather despatch us immediately—Ye executioners, ye inquisitors, does this cruelty proceed from the lenity I shewed to the prisoners I took?—Did it offend you that I treated them with friendship, generosity, honour and humanity?—If it did, our suff'rings will redound more to our honour, and our fall be the more glorious—But remember, this fall will prove your own one day—Wretches! I fear you not, do your worst; and while I here lay suff'ring and chain'd on my back to the damp floor, I'll yet pray for your conversion.[Pg 343]

OFFICER. Excuse us, we have only obey'd our order.

COL. ALLEN. Then I forgive you; but pray execute them.

19

Oh! my lost friends! 'tis liberty, not breath,Gives the brave life. Shun slav'ry more than death.He who spurns fear, and dares disdain to be,Mocks chains and wrongs—and is forever free;While the base coward, never safe, tho' low,Creeps but to suff'rings, and lives on for woe!

[*Exeunt* GUARDS.

SCENE III. *In the Camp at Cambridge.*

GENERAL WASHINGTON, GENERAL LEE, *and* GENERAL PUTNAM.

GENERAL WASHINGTON.

Our accounts from the Northward, so far, are very favourable; Ticonderoga, Chamblee, St. John's and Montreal our troops are already in possession of—and Colonel Arnold, having penetrated Canada, after suff'ring much thro' cold, fatigue and want of provisions, is now before Quebec, and General Montgomery, I understand, is in full march to join him; see these letters.

[*They read.*

GEN. LEE. The brave, the intrepid Arnold, with his handful of fearless troops, have dar'd beyond the strength of mortals—Their courage smil'd at doubts, and resolutely march'd on, clamb'ring (to all but themselves) insurmountable precipices, whose tops, covered with ice and snow, lay hid in the clouds, and dragging baggage, provisions, ammunition and artillery along with them, by main strength, in the dead of winter, over such stupendous and amazing heights, seems almost unparallelled in history!—'Tis true, Hannibal's march over the Alps comes the nearest to it—it was a surprising undertaking, but when compar'd to this, appears but as a party of pleasure, an agreeable walk, a sabbath day's journey.

GEN. PUTNAM. Posterity will stand amazed, and be astonish'd at the heroes of this new world, that the spirit of patriotism should blaze to such a height, and eclipse all others, should outbrave fatigue, danger, pain, peril, famine and even death itself, to serve their country; that they should march, at this inclement season, thro' long and dreary deserts, thro' the remotest wilds, covered with swamps and standing lakes, beset with trees, bushes and briars, impervious to the cheering rays of the sun, where are[Pg 344] no traces or vestiges of human footsteps, wild, untrodden paths, that strike terror into the fiercest of the brute creation.

No bird of song to cheer the gloomy desert!No animals of gentle love's enliven!

GEN. LEE. Let Britons do the like—no—they dare not attempt it—let 'em call forth the Hanoverian, the Hessian, the hardy Ruffian, or, if they will, the wild Cossacks and Kalmucks of Tartary, and they would tremble at the thought! And who but Americans dare undertake it? The wond'ring moon and stars stood aloof, and turn'd pale at the sight!

GEN. WASHINGTON. I rejoice to hear the Canadians received them kindly, after their fatigue furnish'd them with the necessaries of life, and otherways treated them very humanely—And the savages, whose hair stood on end, and look'd and listen'd with horror and astonishment at the relation of the fatigues and perils they underwent, commiserated them, and afforded all the succour in their power.

GEN. LEE. The friendship of the Canadians and Savages, or even their neutrality alone, are favourable circumstances that cannot fail to hearten our men; and the junction of General Montgomery will inspire 'em with fresh ardour.

GEN. PUTNAM. Heavens prosper 'em!

Enter OFFICER *and* EXPRESS.

OFFICER. Sir, here's an Express.

EXPRESS. I have letters to your Excellency.

GEN. WASHINGTON. From whence?

EXPRESS. From Canada, sir.

GEN. WASHINGTON. From the army?

EXPRESS. From the headquarters, sir.

GEN. WASHINGTON. I hope matters go well there.—Had General Montgomery join'd Colonel Arnold when you left it?

EXPRESS. He had, sir—these letters are from both those gentlemen.

[*Gives him the letters.*

GEN. WASHINGTON. Very well. You may now withdraw and refresh yourself, unless you've further to say—I'll dispatch you shortly.

EXPRESS. Nothing further, sir.

[*Exeunt* OFFICER *and* EXPRESS.

[Pg 345]

GEN. WASHINGTON. [*Opens and reads the letter to* GENERALS LEE *and* PUTNAM.] I am well pleased with their contents—all but the behaviour of the haughty Carleton—to fire upon a flag of truce, hitherto unprecedented, even amongst Savages or Algerines—his cruelty to the prisoners is cowardly, and personal ill treatment of General Montgomery is unbecoming a General—a soldier—and beneath a Gentleman—and leaves an indelible mark of brutality—I hope General Montgomery, however, will not follow his example.

GEN. LEE. I hope so too, sir—if it can be avoided; it's a disgrace to the soldier, and a scandal to the Gentleman—so long as I've been a soldier, my experience has not furnish'd me with a like instance.

GEN. PUTNAM. I see no reason why he shou'dn't be paid in his own coin.—If a man bruises my heel, I'll break his head—I cannot see the reason or propriety of bearing with their insults—does he not know it's in our power to retaliate fourfold?

GEN. LEE. Let's be good natur'd, General—let us see a little more of it first——

GEN. PUTNAM. I think we have seen enough of it already for this twelve-months past. Methinks the behaviour of Lord Boston, the ill treatment of poor Allen, to be thrown into a loathsome dungeon like a murderer, be loaded with irons, and transported like a convict, would sufficiently rouse us to a just retaliation—that imperious red coat, Carleton, should be taught good manners—I hope to see him ere long in our College at Cambridge——

GEN. LEE. I doubt; he'll be too cunning, and play truant—he has no notion of learning American manners; ev'ry dog must have his day (as the saying is); it may be our time by and by——the event of war is uncertain——

GEN. PUTNAM. Very true, sir; but don't let us be laugh'd at forever.

Enter an OFFICER *in haste.*

OFFICER. Sir, a messenger this moment from Quebec waits to be admitted.

GEN. WASHINGTON. Let him enter.

[*Exit* OFFICER.

Enter MESSENGER.

GEN. WASHINGTON. What news bring you?[Pg 346]

MESSENGER. I am sorry, sir, to be the bearer of an unpleasing tale——

GEN. WASHINGTON. Bad news have you?—have you letters?

MESSENGER. None, sir—I came off at a moment's warning—my message is verbal.

GEN. WASHINGTON. Then relate what you know.

MESSENGER. After the arrival and junction of General Montgomery's troops with Colonel Arnold's, Carleton was summoned to surrender; he disdaining any answer, fir'd on the flag of truce——

GEN. WASHINGTON. That we have heard—go on.

MESSENGER. The General finding no breach could be effected in any reasonable time, their walls being vastly strong, and his cannon rather light, determined to attempt it by storm—The enemy were apprized of it—however, he passed the first barrier, and was attempting the second, where he was unfortunately killed, with several other brave officers——

GEN. WASHINGTON. Is General Montgomery killed?

MESSENGER. He is certainly, sir.

GEN. WASHINGTON. I am sorry for it—a brave man—I could wish him a better fate!——

GEN. LEE. I lament the loss of him—a resolute soldier——

GEN. PUTNAM. Pity such bravery should prove unsuccessful, such merit unrewarded;—but the irreversible decree of Providence!—who can gainsay?—we may lament the loss of a friend, but 'tis irreligious to murmur at pre-ordination. What happ'ned afterwards?

MESSENGER. The officer next in command, finding their attacks at that time unsuccessful, retired in good order.

GEN. WASHINGTON. What became of Colonel Arnold?

MESSENGER. Colonel Arnold, at the head of about three hundred and fifty brave troops, and Captain Lamb's company of artillery, having in the mean time passed through St. Rocques, attacked a battery, and carried it, tho' well defended, with the loss of some men—

GEN. PUTNAM. I hope they proved more successful.

GEN. LEE. Aye, let us hear.

MESSENGER. The Colonel about this time received a wound in his leg, and was obliged to crawl as well as he cou'd to the hospital, thro' the fire of the enemy, and within fifty yards of the walls, but, thro' Providence, escap'd any further damage.—[Pg 347]—

GEN. PUTNAM. Aye, providential indeed!

GEN. WASHINGTON. Is he dangerously wounded?

MESSENGER. I am told not, sir.

GEN. WASHINGTON. I am glad of it.—What follow'd?

MESSENGER. His brave troops pushed on to the second barrier, and took possession of it.

GEN. WASHINGTON. Very good—proceed.

MESSENGER. A party of the enemy then sallying out from the palace-gate, attacked them in the rear, whom they fought with incredible bravery for three hours, and deeds of eternal fame were done; but being surrounded on all sides, and overpowered by numbers, were at last obliged to submit themselves as prisoners of war.

GEN. PUTNAM. Heav'ns! could any thing prove more unlucky? such brave fellows deserve better treatment than they'll get (I'm afraid) from the inhuman Carleton.

GEN. LEE. Such is the fortune of war, and the vicissitudes attending a military life; to-day conquerors, to-morrow prisoners.

GEN. WASHINGTON. He dares not treat them ill—only as prisoners. Did you learn how those brave fellows were treated?

MESSENGER. It was currently reported in the camp they were treated very humanely.

GEN. WASHINGTON. A change for the better.

GEN. PUTNAM. Produc'd by fear, no doubt from General Montgomery's letter—but no matter from what cause.

GEN. LEE. How far did the remainder of the army retire?

MESSENGER. About two miles from the city, where they are posted very advantageously, continuing the blockade, and waiting for reinforcements.

GEN. LEE. Did the enemy shew any peculiar marks of distinction to the corpse of General Montgomery?

MESSENGER. He was interred in Quebec, with ev'ry possible mark of distinction.

GEN. WASHINGTON. What day did the affair happen on?

MESSENGER. On the last day of the year.

GEN. WASHINGTON. A remarkable day! When was the General interred?

MESSENGER. The second of January.

GEN. LEE. What number of men in the whole attack was killed? did you learn?

MESSENGER. About sixty killed and wounded.[Pg 348]

GEN. WASHINGTON. Have you any thing further to communicate?

MESSENGER. Nothing, sir, but to inform you they are all in good spirits, and desire reinforcements, and heavy artillery may be sent them as soon as possible.

GEN. WASHINGTON. That be our business—with all despatch. You may for the present withdraw. Serjeant!

Enter SERJEANT.

SERJEANT. I wait your order, sir.

GEN. WASHINGTON. See that the Messenger and his horse want for nothing.

SERJEANT. I shall, sir.

[*Exeunt* SERJEANT *and* MESSENGER.

SCENE IV.

GEN. WASHINGTON. I'll despatch an Express to the Congress. This repulse, if I mistake not (or victory, as Carleton may call it), will stand 'em but in little stead—'t will be only a temporary reprieve—we'll reinforce our friends, let the consequence be what it may—Quebec must fall, and the lofty strong walls and brazen gates (the shield of cowards) must tumble by an artificial earthquake; should they continue in their obstinacy, we'll arm our friends with missive thunders in their hands, and stream death on them swifter than the winds.

GEN. LEE. I lament the loss of the valiant Montgomery and his brave officers and soldiers (at this time more especially) 'tis the fortune of war, 'tis unavoidable; yet, I doubt not, out of their ashes will arise new heroes.

GEN. PUTNAM. Who can die a more glorious, a more honourable death than in their country's cause?—let it redouble our ardour, and kindle a noble emulation in our breasts—let each American be determined to conquer or die in a righteous cause.

GEN. WASHINGTON. I have drawn my sword, and never will I sheathe it, till America is free, or I'm no more.

GEN. LEE. Peace is despaired of, and who can think of submission? The last petition from the Congress, like the former, has been disregarded; they prayed but for liberty, peace and safety, and their omnipotent authoritative supreme-ships will grant them neither: War, then, war open and understood, must be resolved on; this, this will humble their pride, will bring their[Pg 349] tyrant noses to the ground, teach 'em humility, and force them to hearken to reason when 'tis too late. My noble General, I join you. [*Drawing his sword.*] I'll away with the scabbard, and sheathe my sword in the bosom of tyranny.

GEN. PUTNAM. Have you not read the speech, where frowning revenge and sounds of awful dread for disgrace at Lexington and loss at Bunker's Hill echo forth? Not smiling peace, or pity, tame his sullen soul; but, Pharaoh-like, on the wings of tyranny he rides and forfeits happiness to feast revenge, till the waters of the red sea of blood deluge the tyrant, with his mixed host of vile cut-throats, murderers, and bloody butchers.

GEN. WASHINGTON. Yet, finding they cannot conquer us, gladly would they make it up by a voluntary free-will offering of a million of money in bribes, rather than be obliged to relish the thoughts of sacrificing their cursed pride and false honour, they sending over to amuse us (to put us off our guard) a score or two of commissioners with sham negotiations in great state, to endeavour to effect, by bribery, deception and chicanery, what they cannot accomplish by force. Perish such wretches!—detested be their schemes!—Perish such monsters!—a reproach to human understanding—their vaunted boasts and threats will vanish like smoke, and be no more than like snow falling on the moist ground, melt in silence, and waste away—Blasted, forever blasted be the hand of the villainous traitor that receives their gold upon such terms—may he become leprous, like Naaman, the Syrian, yea, rather like Gehazi, the servant of Elisha, that it may stick to him for ever.

GEN. PUTNAM. I join you both, and swear by all the heroes of New-England, that this arm, tho' fourscore and four [*Drawing his sword.*], still nervous and strong, shall wield this sword to the last in the support of liberty and my country, revenge the insult offer'd to the immortal Montgomery, and brutal treatment of the brave Allen.

O Liberty! thou sunshine of the heart!Thou smile of nature, and thou soul of art!Without thy aid no human hope cou'd grow,And all we cou'd enjoy were turn'd to woe.

[*Exeunt.*

[Pg 350]

THE EPILOGUE.
SPOKEN BY MR. FREEMAN.

Since tyrants reign, and lust and lux'ry rule;Since kings turn Neroes—statesmen play the fool;Since parli'ment in cursed league combine,To sport with rights that's sacred and divine;Destroying towns with direful conflagration,And murder subjects without provocation!These are but part of evils we could name,Not to their glory, but eternal shame.Petitions—waste paper—great Pharaoh cries,Nor care a rush for your remonstrances.Each Jacobite, and ev'ry pimping Tory,Waits for your wealth, to raise his future glory:Or pensions sure, must ev'ry rascal have,Who strove his might, to make FREEMAN a slave.Since this the case, to whom for succour cry?To God, our swords, and sons of liberty!Cast off the idol god!—kings are but vain!Let justice rule, and independence reign.Are ye not men? Pray who made men, but God?Yet men make kings—to tremble at their nod!What nonsense this—let's wrong with right oppose,Since nought will do, but sound, impartial blows.

Let's act in earnest, not with vain

pretence,

Adopt the language of

sound COMMON SENSE,

And with one voice

proclaim INDEPENDENCE.

Convince your foes you will defend your right,That blows and knocks is all they will get by 't.Let tyrants see that you are well prepar'd,By proclamations, sword, nor speeches scar'd;That liberty freeborn breathe in each soul!One god-like union animate the whole!

End of the First Campaign.

22

Made in the USA
Las Vegas, NV
06 November 2024

11106311R00015